About the

Peter Chainey was a senior legal executive advocate for forty-eight years. He was born on a newly constructed social housing estate in Southampton, three years after the end of the World War II, when rationing still existed. A committed mod in the sixties, he had an appetite for life and pulled himself out of his humble beginnings, despite initially not gaining many GCEs from school, to become a well-known and respected lawyer. A dynamic individual, he founded and chaired the Southampton Civil Litigation Group, as well as being a chairman of Winchester Round Table. Peter is also the successful author of *Legal Time Limits*. Having survived major heart surgery and now suffering from Alzheimer's and vascular dementia, Peter wanted to create a record of his life and achievements. He has been married three times and lives near Winchester, with his third wife, Lizzie. They have been married for twenty-six years.

THE MAN WITH MUD ON HIS BOOTS

Peter Chainey

THE MAN WITH MUD ON HIS BOOTS

Vanguard Press

VANGUARD PAPERBACK

© Copyright 2021
Peter Chainey

A CIP catalogue record for this title is
available from the British Library.

ISBN 978 1 784659 50 9

Vanguard Press is an imprint of
Pegasus Elliot MacKenzie Publishers Ltd.
www.pegasuspublishers.com

First Published in 2021

Vanguard Press
Sheraton House Castle Park
Cambridge England

Printed & Bound in Great Britain

Dedication

This book is dedicated to my beautiful wife, the lady who saved my life, and to my daughters, Emma and Anna.

Prologue

It was 15th December 2012 when I had a heart attack in the middle of the night. I was at home with my wife, Elizabeth (Lizzie) after a day of Christmas shopping, going to the cinema and having a relaxed meal at the end of the day.

I had just gone to bed when a searing pain shot through my chest and traversed along my neck and down my left arm. I shook Lizzie awake, saying that I had a pain in my chest and then blacked out, collapsing on to the bed. I was sixty-four years old and a healthy litigation lawyer.

Lizzie opened my airways, as I had momentarily stopped breathing, and dialled 999. A paramedic arrived quite soon and established that I was having a heart attack. He summoned the ambulance and the next I knew I was in the A & E Unit of Southampton General Hospital. Lizzie was in the ambulance with me. On arrival, I was admitted as an emergency requiring immediate attention. This resulted in a cardiologist inserting an intra-aortic balloon pump to stabilise me, ready for surgery.

For the next two weeks I had to lie down on my back in a ward, as the medics needed to get my triponin levels down in order to operate safely. Lizzie visited me daily and during that time gave me a much clearer picture of what had happened to me on that frightful night.

Eventually, on Christmas Eve, I underwent open heart surgery and had five valves replaced (a quintuple bypass). After this, and my recovery in hospital, my surgeon told me that Lizzie, due to her calmness and quick thinking, had saved my life at the time of the attack by getting me to hospital in 'the golden hour'. From the bottom of my heart I am so grateful to my darling Lizzie who saved my life.

Reflecting on those moments after my discharge from hospital and the long days of recovery to come, I had a distinct awareness of my mortality and a sure knowledge that my life was going to change forever. Certainly, it was going to be of great value to me so that I could cherish every moment with my wife, Lizzie, two daughters, Emma and Anna, and five granddaughters in the years to come.

With that in mind I started to find ways of using my valuable time. Three examples came to mind immediately. Firstly, could I go back to my career as a lawyer after many years of contentious court cases? No, for reasons of stress. Secondly, after researching other careers it was clear I had transferable skills but I felt it daunting to start a new career and all it would entail at this point in my life. Thirdly, I attempted to enrol as a volunteer at the local Citizen's Advice Bureau doing pro-bono work and found that my IT skills were now very slow and it was stressful learning the new systems and practices. In fact, I found many things stressful for my heart and body as a whole. Taking that into consideration I knew the journey of my life would be a challenge but with a difference. Assured of that, I put pen to paper to start and draft the first words of a memoir.

I always enjoyed reading, writing, literacy and history so I set about going through the material I had at home: family photographs, letters, cards and other papers stored in boxes, cupboards, drawers. I also visited relatives who told me their stories to help me start what was going to be an interesting narrative from the outset.

As a writer, author, poet, actor (amateur) and singer (choir baritone/tenor) I give you the story of my life from January 1948, two years after the end of the Second World War and Victory Day in June 1946. It is a true account of love, laughter, loss, tragedy, murder, drama, courage and a remarkable success from this working-class boy.

After my schooling and becoming a young man, I chose a career in law with a local solicitor's office. For the next forty-eight years I became a civil litigation lawyer. From that start, I helped thousands of people to get justice and legal compensation for loss, damage, suffering and any other difficulties in their lives.

The law is an enforceable body of rules that govern any society to provide a standard of procedural fairness and the exact requirements, depending on any context of a problem. As a litigious lawyer I directed my clients through those rules with a clear understanding of care and spirit in the enforcement of their needs to win at the coal face of justice.

Lawyers receive and return a huge amount of correspondence and documents and do a lot of observing, sifting, cataloguing, and cross-referring information as a significant part of their work.

This autobiographical memoir is dedicated to my family and to all of those who are now at peace but not forgotten.

The beginning

On a storm-lashed night in the middle of the winter of 1948, I was born. My birth date was the 4th January and it was a Sunday. My birthplace was a nursing home in Westwood Road, Southampton, Hampshire, England. Evidently, I was a forceps delivery which, at that time, had a very high fatality rate. Thankfully I survived to tell you my tale.

In the same month, Mahatma Ghandi, 'the great soul and man of peace', was assassinated by a Hindu in New Delhi, India. Later in the same year Prince Charles was born into the House of Windsor, to become our future king.

My parents, Dorothy and Leslie Chainey, were young working-class members of a society trying to recover in the austere years following the Second World War under the shadow of rationing until 1954. In the case of my parents, this was compounded by the instability of having to live at a number of different addresses in and around Southampton, before settling in to a permanent home in 1950.

Before that, they lived at my grandparents' terraced house in Commercial Street, Bitterne Village. This had three bedrooms occupied by the family, which swelled up to eight people when my brother, Paul, was born on 26th September 1949. Overcrowded it must have been, bearing in mind there was only one toilet outside and a scullery at the back of the house for all the cooking and washing. I was told years later that at one stage during that time, my parents were facing the threat of homelessness. This all resulted in my brother and I having to live with my mother in her brother, my Uncle John's, house with his family, at Hythe on the other side of Southampton Water.

However, and given these difficulties, it was a great relief for my parents when they moved into Somerset Avenue, Harefield, Southampton. It was on a new council estate, built under the Government's post- war 'homes for heroes' policy. Such homes boasted very modern and comfortable facilities for four people.

On the first floor, there were three spacious bedrooms with built-in wardrobes, together with a family bathroom, having a bath, wash basin and WC. On the ground floor, there was a separate lounge, dining-room and kitchen with plenty of storage space, including cupboards, with numerous work surfaces and room for a cooker and copper tub for all the washing. The larder had a stone block to keep items cool, such as dairy products, including milk and other perishables. The kitchen door opened into a spacious brick outhouse with concrete work surfaces, a large coal bunker and another WC. There was also ample storage room in the loft. In addition, the house was complemented by large gardens in the front and back. Having watched the house being built, my mother's dream of living there really did come true and it would be my parents' home for sixty years.

To complete my immediate family and to bring it up to date, I have a sister named Catherine who was born on 4th September 1966 when I was eighteen years old. She was three years old when I left home to get married. Catherine married Phillip Grafton and they had a boy named Nicholas. Subsequently, following the breakdown of her marriage, and following a divorce, she married Andy Dawkins and had a daughter named Saskia.

Part 1
Childhood memories at a council estate, the end of petrol rationing the loss of Buddy Holly
1950 – 1959

Childhood

Harefield estate was developed initially in the 1830s when Harefield House was built in the style of an Elizabethan manor house. This was eventually purchased by Edwin Jones, a wealthy man with a shop in Southampton, until it was destroyed by fire in 1915. During the 1920s, thirties and forties, there was a limited amount of private housing development on the land until the end of the forties. This was then followed by further extensive council housing developments by the borough councils. During the Second World War, the estate accommodated families evacuated to camps erected during the blitz of Southampton by enemy bombers. As a port and gateway, Southampton was heavily damaged.

Factually, there were fifty-seven enemy attacks on the town, and one thousand six hundred warnings of danger. The Luftwaffe dropped 457 tons of high explosive in the area in 2,361 bombs and 31,000 incendiaries. Casualties were six hundred and thirty dead, eight hundred and ninety-eight seriously hurt and nine hundred and seventy-nine slightly injured. Over four years of the war, 2,653 homes were damaged enough to be demolished, another 8,927 seriously and 32,019 slightly damaged. Two flying bombs (doodle bugs) were also used over the town and the heaviest raid was with fifty bombers. After all that, both King George VI and Prime Minister Winston Churchill (Winnie) visited Southampton to see the damage and to speak with the people to bolster their spirits.

Our new home stood at the end of a terrace of six dwellings which, on its north side, was flanked by an open area of grass leading to Weston Crescent, in which there was a cul-de-sac of about seven private bungalows. On the far side of Weston Crescent and running along Somerset Avenue there were five private detached houses. What the owners of those houses thought of the social housing surrounding them I do not know, but I anticipate there must have been some trepidation. In fact, the children of these properties never played with, or spoke to us, when we were growing up.

The development of the estate was completed with two public houses, a shopping parade and two schools. Initially, the Post Office was in a war-time Nissen hut. Notwithstanding this, the estate was still surrounded by fields and coppices of trees. By the end of the century the population of the estate had grown to 13,711 people.

The new council estate quickly filled up with numerous families and our immediate neighbours were the Arrowsmiths, Zielinskis, Steeges, Webs and Rushes. Further across and along the road were the Parsons, Nichols, Hiltons, Hewitts, Fellows, Sullivans, Zammits, Lawrences, Nosses, Thomases, Tyrells and Swains. Notably, it was a very cosmopolitan cluster of new neighbours seeking the comfort from a post-war shadow.

Quickly, many friendships and acquaintances were made upon which the community could thrive. Such was the trust between everybody there developed a frequent open door policy. For example, neighbours regularly opened each other's doors and enquired if anything was wanted from the local shops, where they were going. This level of trust and friendship was sustained for many years; despite the familiarity the adults always addressed each other Mr and Mrs by surname, out of courtesy.

Before long, Paul and I were in a gang – of the old fashioned type, boys having fun – which in the long days ahead provided opportunities for getting together, knowing each other and setting out on the day's adventures. This was particularly the case on weekends and school holidays. During those times there were no real concerns about safety such as those which now linger over today's youngsters.

Virtually the whole day was used as play time, resulting in us returning home late in the afternoon, famished. Our parents seldom expressed worry or concern as to where we had been or what we had been up to. The estate was relatively safe for boisterous activities, complemented by a great expanse of woodlands and fields where we could, quite literally, lose ourselves. We saw no danger in climbing trees and racing to the top of them irrespective of the possibility we might fall. We would dare each other to run through a large concrete water dispersal pipe running through the copse alongside the road from one end of the estate to the other. Or, we would string a rope to a large tree growing on the side of a sloping bank and, sitting on no more than a short branch tied to the rope, swing out to the highest point, regardless of whether or not the rope or branch would snap in mid-air. It never occurred to us that disaster could happen at any time.

Paul and I simply saw it as having tremendous fun, using our own initiatives, whether it was bold or not. To me it was reminiscent of the adventures of Enid Blyton's *Famous Five* or Arthur Ransome's *Swallows and Amazons*. Our adventures became a constant for the development of our future, which we embraced through the open spaces as if we owned them ourselves, with good feelings of laughter and sunshine. We played cowboys and Indians (I was always on the Indians' side), pirates and sports of football, cricket, rounders and athletics, to let the girls join in with us.

We were always aware that Southampton had a large port, giving us the advantage of seeing the world moving through ships and deliveries of all dimensions. This mesmerised me so much, at a young age, to the extent that my parents bought me *The Dumpy Book of Ships*. I used this every time our family visited Southampton Royal Pier to see big ships like RMS Queen Elizabeth arrive at the Ocean Dock. We always had a picnic in hand. Alas, the pier is no longer there.

Our grandparents

My first and fondest childhood memories included frequent visits to our two sets of grandparents. I always looked forward to seeing them with joy because they were always laughing and giving us sweets and cakes.

My paternal grandparents Chainey lived next to a coal yard where the men's faces and hands were black from the coal dust and for some curious reason they were wearing cutaway sacks on their heads. I also enjoyed watching the coal lorries and horse-drawn carts being loaded up with bags of coal for local deliveries. During the winter months, coal was delivered to our home bunker on Saturdays.

More adventurous was the opportunity for me, at the age of four, to ride bareback on the horses my grandfather looked after for a local farmer, moving them from one field to another on a good day out.

My grandmother always seemed to be at her front garden gate, chatting to the local neighbours. She would say something like, 'Stitchy' Knowlton, a local GP, had visited Mrs Brown and that Bob 'the Coffin', the local undertaker, would not be far behind. Furthermore, she always wore a hat speared with a large hatpin whenever she went shopping. She chuckled all the time.

As to my grandfather, I enjoyed playing board games like chequers with him. His approach to the game ensured he won, although on occasions he would allow me to win, with a wink and knowing smile. He was a quiet man with a big grin and in the winter would look into the fire quietly as if he was watching something.

My Aunt Marg, one of my father's sisters, would take Paul and me to the Sunday school across the road, every week. In the summer each year she would take us, by coach, to Brockenhurst in the New Forest, for a picnic, followed with the Christmas party set up by the Sunday school.

In the case of my maternal Goodridge grandparents, I remember the back garden at their home in Bitterne Park surrounded by a large hydrangea hedge and sloping up to a war-time Anderson shelter at the top, in which Paul and I played whenever the opportunity arose. My mother's father was very dapper and always wore a suit with a bowler hat when going out. Occasionally he would playfully put his hat on our heads. He also had a cane and I would march around the room, bowler on head with the cane slanted on my shoulder just like a soldier, whilst he barked orders.

As for my grandmother, who was always elegant, I remember an occasion when she took me on the bus to town where she bought me a toy lorry loaded with plastic cages containing different species of circus animals, such as lions and bears. Shortly after our return I went to the toilet, still clutching this toy when, suddenly, I dropped the whole lot into the bowl. My grandmother calmly retrieved my toys and cleaned them with no fuss but a smile. I always enjoyed a ride on the top of a bus into Southampton for shopping or watching the boats going up and down the Itchen River into the Solent.

Just before I started my infant school at Bitterne Church of England School in 1953, I made regular visits with my mother to the local health clinic for medication in the form of a red capsule to be taken every day up until and including my first year at primary school. I was then five years old. Sometime later I was told these were cod liver oil capsules for deficiencies in bone structure. I doubt I had rickets, but certainly my legs were a little bit bandy.

In fact I was in good company, because one of my favourite footballers in the fifties was Manuel Francisco dos Santos, otherwise known as Garrincha (little bird), who played for Brazil and could bend a ball into the net long before David Beckham.

One of the things I dreaded was a visit to the dentist. The surgery was situated in an old house surrounded by a bomb site in the middle of Southampton. The dentists worked on my teeth with a drill connected to and driven by a foot pedal. It would grind away with a whirring noise which for me seemed to be an unbearable length of time. The noise was like the scratching of a teacher's nail being dragged across a blackboard.

The only advantage to these visits for my brother and me, was that our mother would do some shopping in town while we played games on the bomb sites with other children. There were quite a few of these still scattered across Southampton but, by 1955, many new buildings had sprung up very quickly to mend the wounds the town and its people had suffered during the war.

Before I started school in 1953, my mother tuned in to the radio in the afternoon to hear the BBC broadcasting stories for children including the popular *Listen with Mother* presented by Daphne Oxenford. As a family, my parents regularly listened to the radio throughout the fifties for the daily news, sport and entertainment such as Billy Cotton's *Workers Playtime*, *The Goon Show*, *Dick Barton*, *Dragnet*, *Quatermass* and sport. This set the standards for a new generation, not only for the nation, but for radio and television as well. Both of these were monopolised by the BBC (with two TV channels), but not everybody had a TV set, my parents included. Times were about to change.

In 1953 the government approved and set in motion commercial television as a rival to the BBC. This created Channel 3 as a new ITV network in the London area in 1955. The age of information technology was ready to expand and develop a new means of sound and vision to educate the world widely upon the dawn of an exciting future.

Throughout my life, I have harboured an affection for the world of words, particularly the writing and reading of books. Their layout and meanings, whether as stories, entertainment or educational, could engage my mind for hours.

As a feature of this, Paul and I looked forward to our journeys to the local library with our parents where we could broaden our knowledge in a number of ways. Added to that, our home was abundant with volumes from book clubs. All of this could be complemented by the radio and later the TV.

Before long, our home was cluttered with comics and books, such as *Eagle, Beano, Dandy, Roy of the Rovers* (I still have my 1959 annual), with characters such as Dan Dare and Digby, Roy Race and Dennis the Menace. Over a period of time I took a great interest in collecting American comics such as those published by Dell and DC, which not only introduced me to characters such as Superman, Batman and Spiderman, but also non-fiction biographies of frontiersmen, Daniel Boone and Davy Crockett. Combined with these were novels like *The Last of the Mohicans* and *The Red Badge of Courage* (about the American Civil War, which helped the book I would write later). This made me start a great interest in all things American, particularly the history of North American Indians (now referred to as Native Americans). Indeed, at fifteen years old I wrote and illustrated a book called The United States of America, a comprehensive history of the US from 1765 to 1963. I still have this, written in biro in a lined exercise book of one hundred and forty-four pages!

In addition, as children, every Saturday morning we went with our friends to the Ritz cinema in Bitterne to watch the Saturday matinees. There we could see our favourite stars such as Roy Rogers, Hopalong Cassidy and Gene Autry, as well as the popular cartoons, Sylvester the cat, Tweety-pie the bird and Tom and Jerry plus comedians such as the Three Stooges.

At one of these matinees, when I was eight years old, I responded to a request for volunteers to sing a song on stage. I went on the stage to give my rendition of Guy Mitchell's song, *Singing the Blues*, which was top of the pop chart at the time. For this, I was rewarded with a large jamboree bag of various sweets. The manager of the cinema said I had a good pitch and strong voice. Little did I know this performance was to be the beginning of my future career on the stage in years to come. At the time, my friends and I had a good feast of the jamboree bag of sweets.

On another occasion, at a matinee, Roy Rogers, my cowboy hero, was about to see off the bandits, when one of my friends cried out that he wanted to go home. On being asked why, he plaintively cried that he had just pushed an aniseed ball up his nose and couldn't get it out. Why he put it there we never knew, but we got him home, after which he was rewarded with having his Adenoids surgically removed. We certainly weren't going to put our fingers up his snotty nose.

Further enjoyment in my formative years was to be found in going to the cinema at Southampton during school holidays to see classic technicolour films such as *Spartacus*, *Twenty Thousand Leagues Under The Sea*, *Moby Dick* and *The Alamo* (amongst many others) usually at the Odeon or ABC cinemas. The ABC had an organist who just before the start of the feature film would rise from the pit playing away with a big grin on his face which he maintained throughout his performance, to be met with a chorus of boos and hisses until he descended back into the pit, still smiling.

Whilst mentioning films seen as children, we also went to the cinema in the evenings with our parents, when we were older, to see films, largely about the Second World War, in which both my parents were involved. My father was in the Royal Navy based at Portsmouth and my mother in the Civil Defence Corps as an ambulance driver in Southampton. They liked films such as *Reach for the Sky*, *Sink the Bismark*, *The Longest Day* and many others of that genre. Equally, our mother would take Paul and me to see *Gone with the Wind*, *Brief Encounter* and *The King and I* in the school holiday afternoons.

One outcome of this was that when my mother and I were in Plummers department Store, Southampton, I saw a lady with red painted fingernails. Upon seeing this I asked my mother, innocently, if the lady was a film star, because I had only seen varnished nails in films. My mother, who never wore coloured nail polish explained gently that the lady was not a film star.

Overall, I have become an avid follower of films from any culture and genre worldwide. I now also enjoy being able to watch films on DVD at home. Lizzie and I are members of Harbour Lights Cinema in Southampton and have sometimes been known to see films back to back. Interestingly, since marrying Lizzie, I have never had a TV at home.

Hit by a car

In the spring of 1953, at the age of five, I had an accident near home. This happened on a Sunday lunchtime. I had crossed the road in front of our house to buy a bag of crisps from a grocery van parked on the other side of the road. Having got the crisps, I jumped out of the opened door of the back of the van and was hit by a passing car. When I opened my eyes I was in the back of an ambulance with my father, and could hear a bell ringing. I then went to sleep.

The next time I opened my eyes I saw my mum and dad with a nurse. They told me I was in Southampton Children's Hospital, with a bandage around my head. They then told me what had happened to me and that I had a wound in the right side of my temple near to the eye socket. I was informed that I would be in hospital for a few days.

Whilst I was in hospital the coronation of Queen Elizabeth II took place on 2nd June 1953 in Westminster Abbey. All the patients in the children's ward were given a small tin box with knobs on the top and bottom with which we could scroll along a coloured picture of the coronation procession, including the queen's coach and red-coated soldiers.

Upon my discharge from the hospital I was able, with my family, to join in with the coronation celebrations set up in our street, with a party clad with flags and bunting and at which all the children were given a commemorative drinking glass with a royal crown on it. I am pleased to say that I still have mine. It was a very grand and memorable day, full of food, drinks and many people having a good time. So much so, one of our neighbours, Mr Fellows, turned up dressed as Santa Claus to add more to the enjoyment!

It was estimated that twenty million people watched this occasion by television. Furthermore, the live ceremonial pictures created a new style of communication for the world and the future. As for my accident,

I fully recovered and was left with just a small scar. This all happened in the year I started school.

About twelve years ago at a party, one of the Tyrell boys (they were neighbours with whom we used to play as friends) approached me and said he was with me when my accident happened. He told me what happened and that my poor father was hysterical, distraught and raving that I was not alive, as I lay, bloodied and unconscious, in the gutter. Apparently, a policeman was cycling up the same road, saw the accident and administered first aid to me. Because of that and the ambulance service quickly coming to the scene, my life was saved!

As we were getting older on the estate, nicknames became common and in some cases everlasting such as 'Farts', which was, and still is, laughable in contrast to the offensive, obscene and damaging language of youngsters today. Contrasted with today, we seldom swore at each other due mainly to the respect we had for each other, our parents and being put right by our elders. It was meant to be in fun those days.

Besides that, we had enough time to let off steam in the enjoyment of playing games together such as football, cricket, rounders, hop scotch, hide-and-seek, cowboys and Indians and athletic races round the block. We also raced home-made wooden go-carts along the pavements, fields and copses, sometimes wrecking them in crashes and attempting to repair them as quickly as possible. Great fun, and all innocent pastimes. On reflection, these were character building to strengthen us, both physically and mentally, to deal with the challenges before us.

Not so innocent was the making of small mud pies in our back gardens and flicking these on sticks over our roofs, having no idea where they might land. Unfortunately, on one occasion Paul lobbed a mud pie straight through our bathroom window, upon which he said, "The old chap's not going to like that". True to form, our father made us clean up the mess in the bathroom and docked our pocket money for one month.

Undeterred, we had fun attaching a long piece of string to a door-knocker and then hiding behind bushes, pulling the string and watching the neighbours opening their doors together. The neighbours would shout out, "You wicked boys. We know who you are and are going to tell your parents!"

Another activity was scrumping apples from gardens. Unfortunately, on one occasion I had climbed a tree and was happily picking and throwing apples down to my brother and a friend when it suddenly went very quiet. That silence was broken by a man's voice bellowing, "What do you think you're doing, my lad?" Before I could respond he told me to get down from his tree and made me collect up every apple that had fallen in his large orchard. There were loads of them! Somewhat crestfallen, I got home late that afternoon and received a stern, "Serves you right," from my parents.

That however did not quench our thirst for adventure because shortly thereafter one of the older boys from another gang further up the road produced an air rifle and peppered the green knickers of a neighbours' daughter with pellets as they hung on their washing line. We scarpered very quickly!

Furthermore, and somewhat dangerously, we developed an induction ceremony to join our band of friends. This consisted of us digging a shallow trench in a copse, upon which we would lay a corrugated steel panel under which we expected a potential new member to lie, whilst we lobbed stones onto the steel cover. We would do this counting up to ten and, if the new member sustained the onslaught, he would be judged fit to be inducted. Unfortunately, one potential member couldn't sustain it, ran home in tears, told his father what we were doing and that was the end of that, with the father chasing us.

There were also other amusing moments. On a summer's day we were playing outdoors and saw a Robin Reliant three-wheeler motor car coming down one of the estate roads quite fast when, in attempting to turn into the main road, it suddenly rolled over on to its roof. We watched this, open-mouthed, and started laughing. We ran over to see the driver was upside down and struggling to get out of his seat. We asked if he was all right, whereupon he said, "No, I'm not all right, so bugger off." Quickly, two men arrived and helped the driver out of his car, having noted that he was not injured. Feeling a little manly, we joined in with lifting the car back on to its wheels. Still mumbling and swearing, the red-faced driver went off, without any words of gratitude.

On another occasion, we were playing cricket on the green alongside our house, as was usual on a summer's evening, when one of us batted the soft ball into the stairwell of a passing bus where it continued bouncing around, much to the surprise of the startled passengers. Suffice to say, we made ourselves scarce very quickly as the bus conductor came rushing back to give us a real rollicking. When he had gone we continued playing the game as if nothing had happened.

Later in the summer 1959, my brother fell off the outhouse roof at home during a game with friends and fractured a number of fingers on his hand. Needless to say, he went to hospital and we were never allowed to play that game again!

Generally, we had plenty of freedom to do very much what we wanted, wandering as far as we could go without care along narrow lanes, meandering through the countryside, crossing vast acres of fields with stunning views, climbing trees (to see who could be the first to the top), and seeking out streams where we would try and catch newts, minnows, sticklebacks and frogs.

As time moved on, we acquired our own forms of transport to expand our horizons, by cycling to outlying villages, which before we could only access by an infrequent bus service. This allowed us many more hours of freedom under what seemed to be an everlasting sun.

One of our journeys in the school holidays was to Eastleigh Airport on a warm evening. This was usually to wash the detritus, such as dead birds, off the wings of small planes. We were only about fourteen to sixteen years old and didn't mind not being paid because we were more interested in the planes. One year, Hughie Green, the TV show man, flew in to the airport in his own plane and we washed his wings. We were chuffed.

Sadly, all of this was starting to change as we watched with concern our open spaces disappearing under expanding new developments. These were about to destroy and swallow up our precious vestiges of childhood forever.

Overall, my childhood was very happy in what seemed to be an unending period of adventure, discovery, friendship, fun and laughter without any regrets, and all of which I believe enabled me to develop my character in a positive way for the future. This was initially reflected in me by joining the Life Boys and then the 21st Itchen Scouts Troop.

Added to this, and from my heart, I owe an enormous debt to my parents who, in great measure, provided the infrastructure, encouragement and support of a safe and stable environment, full of love, laughter and good values.

In September 1959, I started at Merry Oak Secondary Technical Boys' School where I would be for the next five years of my life.

Earlier that year, the world was shaken when, on the 3rd February 1959, my favourite American pop singer, Buddy Holly, died in a plane crash at Iowa, USA. He was twenty-two, and considered to be magnetic and prolific, and to this day is a powerful icon in the world of popular music. His inimitable style was expounded through classical songs such as *That'll be the day*, *Listen to me*, *Peggy Sue*, *Every Day* and *Oh Boy* and has been copied by millions of musicians, including The Beatles, Rolling Stones, Kinks, Small Faces, Sex Pistols and other ground-breaking, well- known followers of this genre. From my early teens I was one of those followers. One of my treasures is a first edition of *Buddy Holly and the Crickets Album of Popular Song Hits including Words, Music, Tonic Sol-Fa & Guitar Chords*" by James J. Kriegsmann in 1957. I still sing the songs from the album, sometimes with a choir, to make me feel full of life and to remember: 'The music still goes on'.

Part 2
My parents and their ancestries

A Chainey Wedding

A Chainey Wedding

My parents and their ancestries

Before I deal with this in some detail, I flag up at this stage sincere thanks to my cousin, Anne-Marie Barker, who, over a number of years, researched and eventually produced family trees dedicated to my mother's side of the family, dating back to 1727. Furthermore, much help was given to me by my mother to enable me to construct a full and factual picture of her lifetime. Without their help, I would have struggled to develop and write an informed narrative. Despite my efforts and in contrast, no proper family tree exists to my knowledge dedicated to my father's side. I have therefore constructed and written such a narrative to the best of my ability and knowledge from other members of the family, especially my Uncle Maurice Weavers, with family photographs. Thank you all.

My mother

Dorothy Irene Goodridge was born on 13th September 1922 at Hillside Avenue, Bitterne Park, Southampton, her family home. My mother's birth certificate recorded that her father was Cecil Sydney Goodridge, an insurance agent, and her mother was Mary Ellen May Goodridge, formerly Warren, a housewife (but more of that later).

My mother was one of eleven siblings who survived after birth, namely in order, Cecilia (Cissie), Cecil, Bessie (Dibby), Alf, John, May, Frank, Frederick (Fred), Mary and Pamela. Sadly, there were in addition twins who died at birth. In all, fourteen children were born over a period of twenty-two years. In this time big families were the norm. Tuberculosis was common and if they survived it was hoped that the children would get a job and help with the domestic purse. Historically, in 1929 Alexander Fleming discovered the miracle drug, penicillin, a great moment for the health of people all over the world when it came into use in the 1940s. At some stage in her teens, my mother broke an ankle at the ice rink in Southampton. She soon recovered.

Her home on Hillside Avenue was a large detached Victorian house with a scullery and kitchen boasting a large iron range. There was still gas lighting, but no electricity for some time and I often saw my grandmother heating water on the range for ironing and cooking and using candles at bedtime.

Sleeping arrangements were more than one to a bed and in her case, my mother shared a bed with her sister, May. The girls said that the house was haunted because one night she and May were woken to see the misty image of a woman standing over them. Somehow the family could sleep but, I suspect, with some discomfort. Goodness knows what would happen when the girls and boys were getting older.

I was told that life with my grandfather, Cecil Goodridge, was at times very strict and regimented (he was a sergeant-major during the war), particularly on Sundays when the whole family would attend church for the morning service, after which he would set out with his chums to the local pub, returning in the afternoon to a hungry brood waiting for him to return before they could eat.

That said, my mother told me on many occasions that she had a happy childhood and education at Bitterne Park School, where she excelled in English, especially spelling (as I did). That happiness during the 1920s and 1930s was not only with her family but also through a number of friendships, the closest of which was with her friend Phylis (called Phyl) who lived nearby. So close was their friendship that it lasted all through my mother's lifetime. Phyl was such a good a friend that she helped my mother to recover when she broke her ankle, while they were skating together.

They were also both keen cyclists and, as they grew older, they would frequently cycle from Southampton to places like the New Forest and, in summertime, Lee-on-Solent, to relax by the sea. This was evident from some postcards I found sent to my mother during the 1930s giving a picture and flavour of the good times she had during those years.

Incidentally, the school leaving age at the time was fourteen. Thus, in the Goodridge family, it was expected that, having reached that age, the children would need to find work to assist in financing the household budget. In the case of the girls, that expectation normally translated into domestic service with local, more prosperous, families. This is precisely what happened to my aunts, Cissie and Dibby.

In my mother's case, she went to work in a bakery shop in 1936 where May, her sister, was a manageress. There were two such shops in East Street and Bedford Place, both owned by the Southwell family. I believe my mother alternated between each of them, travelling by bike or tram. Interestingly, amongst my mother's papers was an employer's reference dated 28th April 1939, written to her in glowing terms. Mary actually left school at fourteen years of age and worked in a chemist shop.

Similarly, with the boys, Cecil jr. went to work at the Post Office (where I believe my grandfather also worked sometimes), John joined the Territorial Army as a despatch rider, Alf became a Scaffolder and Frank joined the Royal Navy. Fred, the youngest, eventually became a despatch rider with the ARP (Air Raid Patrol) when the Second World War broke out.

When my mother left school in 1936 a number of events unfolded which changed the landscape of the country, not the least of which was the abdication of King Edward V111 in December. That was to enable the king to marry Mrs Wallis Simpson, an American divorcee (a scandal at the time) and avoid a constitutional crisis, bearing in mind discontent and despair amongst the nation elsewhere.

This was demonstrated by the Jarrow March by workers from the north of England, Jarrow-on-Tyne to be precise, a distressed area and community in despair through unemployment and extreme poverty. The two hundred marchers (known as the Jarrow Crusade) delivered a petition to parliament signed by more than eleven thousand people. The irony of this was that the economy of Jarrow was shortly to be boosted by the Second World War.

More alarmingly for the continent of Europe, the German Army marched into the Rhineland in breach of the Treaty of Versailles made after the First World War. France was again being threatened. Equally, the Italian Army used poison gas and bombed defenceless villages, when marching upon Addis Ababa in Abyssinia. Mussolini proclaimed that Italy had 'her empire'.

At about the same time, a right-wing revolt erupted in Spain headed by General Franco against a popular front of the liberal and left wing parties. Vicious fighting soon spread throughout the country into a civil war, embracing some international elements, notably the International Brigades. This all enabled Germany and Italy to show a display of military might; for example, in the case of Germany, new Condor bombers were used to blitz the Spanish mainland, destroying many towns, including Guernica, with great loss of lives.

Other countries could only watch with trepidation and horror, because the stoking of the fire would become the ferocious hell of World War Two.

The orphans of Guernica in Southampton

Following the bombing of Guernica, Spain by the Condor Legions, the British government agreed to send fleets of ships to evacuate the children of the Spanish town to safety, many of whom had been orphaned. As a deep water port, Southampton was able to accommodate many of those ships. After docking, the children were billeted in tents and huts on the playing fields in and around Southampton, mainly at Stoneham near to my mother's home. She told me that when riding through the town she saw the pitiful movement of many children, day and night. Some of those children eventually stayed in Southampton, whilst others were dispersed throughout the country. Equally, some went back to Spain, but mainly after their war. In commemoration of these events there is a memorial to these children at Stoneham, on the outskirts of the town.

After these occurrences, the nation started to feel the danger of another war. In their home, my grandfather predicted, correctly, that Hitler was intent on starting another war to avenge their humiliation and defeat in the First World, 'the war to end all wars', in which he took part.

That prediction became a reality, when in 1939 German Forces invaded Czechoslovakia and Poland, in breach of the 1938 Munich Agreement. In his address to the nation by radio on 3rd September 1939, Prime Minister Neville Chamberlain declared that, in consequence of Hitler's refusal to withdraw his forces from Poland, Great Britain was at war with Germany.

My mother remembered these ominous events very clearly and told me that the mood was one of apprehension linked to a strong feeling of national unity, resulting in an attitude that 'what had to be done must be done'. In my mother's case this was to open up new chapters in her life which would mould her future, both with her first love, tragedy and then second love everlasting. The first of these developed from a chivalrous soldier named Len. He was tall, handsome but shy and wanted to buy some cakes from the shop where she was the manager.

Corporal Leonard Thomas Biss, a true king's warrior

Lenonard Thomas Biss lived at 'Earlville', Wembury near Plymouth, Devon. He was born in 1920 and became a Corporal in the 1st Field Squadron Royal Engineers Regiment (REME) of the British Army. He was a regular soldier travelling the world with his regiment (for example to Chingwayo's Kraal, Zululand) both before and after hostilities started in Europe. As a member of the 1st Field Squadron, he was involved in the laying and clearance of land mines and other such dangerous ordnance.

Len went with another soldier to get the cakes from a bakery in Southampton where my mother worked. The next day he and his friend returned to the shop and being shy, Len got his friend to ask my mother if she would like to go out with him. After some laughter and thought my mother said, "Yes." From then on they embarked upon a wonderful romance, which quickly blossomed into an engagement.

After war was declared, Len's regiment was immediately mobilised for action. During that difficult time there were scant periods of leave, which enabled my mother and Len to enjoy precious time together, including at least one visit to Len's family in Plymouth. There, she met his mother and father, Annie and Frederick Biss, and his brother who was in the Royal Navy. In the distance the drums of war were rumbling.

In September 1940, the Italian Tenth Army crossed the Libyan border into Egypt. This was at a time when the Battle of Britain was reaching a climax and Germany had not yet committed the full weight of its army to North Africa (it had sent a relatively small force to assist the Italians) for the simple reason that Hitler was more interested in occupying Greece.

Following defeat in the Battle of Britain and with the British and Commonwealth Armies having destroyed the bulk of the Italian Tenth Army, the Germans sent one of their best generals to the Middle East.

His name was Erwin Rommel and he arrived in Tunis in February 1941 to take command of the newly formed Afrika Korps. Things were about to change and reinforcements were required to bolster the Allied Armies. The Middle East Expeditionary Force was formed and made ready to go to North Africa. This included Len's regiment.

My mother and her first husband, Leonard Bliss,
on their wedding day

In consequence of events, on 20th August 1941 my mother and Len were married at the Church of the Ascencion, Bitterne Park, Southampton, witnessed by my mother's father, mother, brother-in-law George (Cissie's husband) and Len's mother. My mother immediately became Mrs Dorothy Biss. A short honeymoon was spent by the newly-weds at Melksham village in Wiltshire and, in September 1941 Len set sail with his regiment for Egypt. I cannot but feel that it was a very emotional time for the families and particularly my mother, knowing that Len was going into battle and hoping with all her young heart that he would return. After some success by the Allied Armies at the siege of Tobruk, and the sinking of some enemy supply ships there was a lull at the end of 1941. It did not last for long.

At the beginning of 1942 the British Army did not know that Rommel was planning a counter-offensive; the date for this was set at

21st January. Logistically, but unfortunately, the position on the ground at the beginning of the year was that the British Army was far from its supply base, whereas, the Afrika Korps were dangerously near their main base. Thus, when it came, the counter-attack by Rommel on the 21st January, supported by many tanks, was ferocious, rapid and unrelenting in its deadly purpose of quickly breaching the British Army forward lines. This resulted into a conflagration of havoc and huge loss of life, including that of Corporal Len. It was the first battle of El Alamein.

It was not until she received a letter dated 23rd February 1942 from the Royal Engineers Record Office that my mother received a formal message of the loss of Len, confirming that he was 'killed in action', followed by a further letter from Buckingham Palace expressing the sympathy and gratitude of King George VI and the queen 'for a life so nobly given'. My mother was crushed, as were all members of the families involved. Len was only twenty-one years old and my mother nineteen. Tragically, this was a terrible blow of fate. Shortly afterwards my mother received Len's personal effects which included his wallet containing a beautiful photograph of my mother. For the next year my mother went into deep mourning, supported by her family.

My mother's loss was further compounded after the war, on two counts. First, she received news that Len's brothers had both been lost in action during the war. Then, much later, in a letter from the Commonwealth War Graves Commission, my mother was told that there was no grave for Len, but simply a citation in his name on the Alamein Memorial in Egypt. I obtained a copy of this for my mother. Over the years my mother often pondered about making a visit to the memorial, but she never did. Before she died my mother gave Len's wallet to me as well as his bible and wonderful photographs of two young people named Mr and Mrs Biss enjoying themselves with smiles of love and laughter.

As a footnote, it could be said that the action of Len's sacrifice was not in vain, for the Eighth Army under the leadership of General Bernard Montgomery went on to defeat the German Army at the final battle of El Alamein in October 1943. This became one of the most significant turning points towards defeating Germany and bringing the war to an end. In achieving that Len was a true hero.

The Goodridge family go to war

As expected, and from his experiences as a soldier in the First World War, as well as being head of the household, my grandfather mobilised his family to deal with the future trials and tribulations of a nation at war.

One of the first priorities in 1939 was the building of an Anderson shelter at the top of the garden at 1 Hillside Avenue, the family home, in the event of any air-raids. The shelter would not survive a direct hit but it would give some cover and comfort to the family, nonetheless.

My mother told me that during an air raid the family would squeeze into the shelter until the raid was finished. The most difficult nights were those when the enemy would bomb Southampton and the docks just before midnight and then return on a second raid just before daybreak so that there was little rest or comfort for the people. There was certainly much discomfort on cold and wet nights huddled up in the shelters, resulting in many health problems. Fred, my mother's youngest brother, suffered with rheumatoid arthritis for the rest of his life, although whether it was caused by these conditions is unknown.

The sounds of an impending air raid quickly became familiar to my mother and her family. It would start with the air-raid sirens winding-up followed almost immediately by the sound of heavy gunfire from ack-ack artillery, and then the ominous whistle and loud blast of the enemy bombs.

Amid this crescendo of sounds and fear could be heard the hum of the German aircraft engines. On some nights the family would stand outside their shelter and from the elevated height of their garden watch Southampton burning. On one such night, an ammunition ship exploded in the docks, sending exploded ordnance in all directions and lighting up the sky for many hours, thus providing an unfortunate beacon of light for the next string of bombers to drop their deadly loads.

My mother said that the most threatening sound was that of the V1 doodlebugs (pilotless winged bombs) because when the engine cut out you knew that it was going to crash to earth, but where, nobody would know until it exploded.

During each blitz of Southampton, my mother was an ambulance driver with the Civil Defence Corps, and she could witness, close up, the devastation and horrendous casualties rendered by the bombing. On one occasion, she was driving towards the centre of Southampton, when an air raid started and a stick of bombs dropped all the way down London Road along which she was driving. She had to stop her vehicle to help others, including people injured by the blasts.

On another occasion two German bombers flew very low on a daylight raid by meandering along the contours of the River Itchen on their way to bomb the Supermarine works at Woolston (where parts for Spitfire aircraft were being manufactured). She actually saw one of the planes being shot down as it attempted to fly away, having dropped its bombs. My mother told me that she saw no parachutes as the plane dived into Southampton Water.

American soldiers in Southampton

Following the Japanese attack on Pearl Harbour in December 1941, the United States of America declared a state of war against Japan and Germany. By August 1942 American troops had arrived in England in readiness for the assault on Europe, which would inevitably come. Although based largely in Devon and Dorset, some American units were billeted in and around Southampton, particularly in readiness for D-Day in June 1944. These units included large contingents of combat GIs.

Some of these troops visited my mother's confectionary shop and purchased large quantities of cakes and other delicacies to distribute at parties put on by them frequently for the benefit of the local communities and children. One of the GIs, named Wayne Alley, was a frequent visitor to the cake shop and started dating my mother's friend, Phylis called Phyl. Wayne was an assault engineer and eventually took part in the invasion of Omaha Beach on D-Day.

He was not heard of for some time. Then out of the blue, Wayne contacted Phyl with a marriage proposal. Phyl was delighted to accept this (and my mother was thrilled for her!) and eventually set sail for New York to be met on arrival by Wayne. He had paid her fare for the passage. They were married on 25th July 1946 and set up home in Pueblo, Colorado, where they happily raised their family of two boys and two girls (more of which I deal with later). Over the years my mother and Phyl corresponded regularly and when she came back to England to see her family she always made a point of visiting my mother for a joyful reunion. Their friendship was to last until my mother passed away.

As for my mother's siblings, May joined the Women's Auxiliary Air Force (WAAF) working on barrage balloons; Cecil was rescued with other members of the British Army at Dunkirk; John was captured at Singapore and put to work on the Siam railway (where he suffered much brutality at the hands of his Japanese captors); Alf was stationed in Beirut with his regiment; and Frank continued to serve in the Royal Navy. Fred ended up in the ARP. Luckily, all of the brothers and sisters returned from battle and were able to resume their lives.

Uncle Fred and a bomb in his pocket

In 1941 when Southampton was still being blitzed by German air raids, young Uncle Fred was walking along a river's edge and spotted several unexploded incendiary bombs. He was always looking for souvenirs, such as shrapnel, and thought this to be a good catch. The problem was that he could only put one bomb in his trousers! Having cleaned the whole bomb, he put it in the front of his trousers, under his belt, to hide it, nose upwards. Fearing that the local bobby or any other adult might think he looked suspicious and confiscate the bomb, he got it home safely. As to the other bombs, he found out later that some had an anti-personnel charge in them.

Young and adventurous as he was, when the Battle of Britain was in full action, Uncle Fred would sit on the top of Midanbury Hill and watch the great air battles in the sky above. From his position he could also watch Spitfire and Hurricane planes re-fuelling and going back up into the fray in the skies over Southampton including Eastleigh airport. Historically, the first Spitfire flew from Eastleigh after production at the Supermarine factory, Woolston thereby helping that part of World War 2 as needed. Unfortunately, during an air raid from the Luftwaffe, the factory suffered a direct hit killing many people. Supermarine then moved their factory to the Midlands.

As an interesting footnote, during the war my mother received a German PostKarte dated 24-6-43, sealed by the German and English authorities, from a prisoner of war named Jim Gosling at Heydebreck POW Camp, and written in pencil, stating that he was from Southampton. Furthermore, he mentioned 'prison life' and concluded with the words, 'I would like to hear from you as I do not hear from the old country often'. I do not know if my mother ever sent a reply. I still have the card.

Much has been suggested recently by so-called modern historians that Winston Churchill's famous war-time speeches did not inspire the nation. Some years ago, I discussed this with my father and mother when

I was reading a book about Churchill and they said that in their views and those of their families, the strength of purpose in those speeches in the darkest days of the war inspired in people the hope of achieving victory. We did achieve victory, against the odds and in the most dire and dangerous of circumstances. At the most critical time, Winston Churchill was under constant pressure from his coalition government to surrender and appease Hitler, but he had the strength of will and foresight to resist, as the outcome for the world in doing otherwise was unthinkable.

After the war, my mother continued working in the confectionary shop, cycling to and from work each day and regularly supplying her family with cakes at weekends. Before too long, my mother's bicycle was to be at the centre of an event which was to change her life forever.

My mother's ancestry with a touch of Français

Earlier, I mentioned my mother's family tree. This is complemented by a dateline for the Warren and Goodridge families. There are a number of interesting features in respect of both families.

There appears to be a strong French connection, centred on Britanny and Jersey, on the Warren side of my mother's family. The evidence for this rests with the inclusion of ancestors named Jeanneton Esther Perchard, Nancy LeQuesne and Mary Ann Seelleur. All are linked to John Warren, a name repeated throughout the family tree from 1795 and 1865 when my great-grandfather of the same name was born. My great-great-grandfather married a French woman, Jeanneton Perchard (without the name Esther) in 1841. My great-grandfather, John Warren, married Mary Ellen Corley from St. Brieuc, Britanny, in 1890. She was related to the Journeau and Le Canu families, but there is very little further information about these, except that a Violet Journeau visited my grandparents sometime before the Second World War. This is shown on a family photograph taken at Hillside Avenue. Their daughter, Mary Ellen May Warren (my grandmother) was born in 1892. In her childhood, my mother met some of her French relatives when they came to Hillside Avenue.

A different cup of tea

My great-grandfather, John Warren, was an accomplished Mariner and crewed many vessels including the tea baron Sir Thomas Lipton's J Class yacht *Shamrock*, which competed in the America Cup races at least five times between 1899 and 1930. He also crewed the steam yachts *Titania* and *Majesta*, owned and sailed by Claude Graham-White, a well-known pioneer of aviation who, in 1910, was the first aviator to make a flight in the night.

J. Lipton and John Warren on board J Class yacht, *Shamrock*

The Goodridges and an alias named 'Windebank'

The earliest known date for the Goodridge family is the marriage of Francis Goodridge to Elizabeth Over. Their descendant, John Goodridge, was born in 1832 and he married Mary Oak (born 1835) in 1855. Their son, Alfred John Goodridge was born in 1856 and he married Hannah Tibbles (born 1858) in 1878. Their son, Cecil Sydney Goodridge (my mother's father), was born in 1887.

There were three Goodridge great uncles, William, born in 1864, Frank, born in 1870 and Matthew, born in 1876, together with another relative named Alfred Henry Goodridge. They all joined the British Army, enlisting in the Dorset Regiment, 1st Hampshire Regiment, Royal Artillery and 3rd Hampshire Regiment respectively. My grandfather Goodridge ran away from home in 1903 and joined the British Army, Dorsetshire Regiment, 10th Mounted Infantry. He was barely fifteen years old and therefore used an alias, 'Alfie Windebank'. He also gave his false family address as Oak Tree Road, Bitterne Park, Southampton. It later transpired that there really was an Alfie Windebank living in the same road.

Shortly after joining the army, my grandfather was in trouble with his regiment. In September 1903, he overstayed his pass by eight hours fifty-five minutes and was admonished. A little time later, after he had been posted to Dorchester, he overstayed his pass by one day five hours and was confined to barracks for seven days. On 27th May 1904 he was admonished again for having a dirty rifle and was further confined to barracks for three days. On the 15th June the following year he again overstayed his pass by three hours fifty minutes and was confined to barracks for seven days. I can only hazard a guess as to what he was getting up to, but it was most certainly not anything to do with the British Army.

In any event, after three years' service he was transferred to the Army Reserve. According to a Christmas greetings card from my grandfather dated 1909 his address was 'Dundee', Oak Tree Road.

Shortly after, in 1910, my grandparents got married just five days before their first child, Cecilia (my Aunt Cissie),was born. At that time they were living with John and Mary Warren, in Hillside Avenue.

World War 1

Due to events in the Balkans and the Teutonic invasion of Belgium, against the protestations of Great Britain and France, war broke out on the 14th August 1914 with a very belligerent Germany, which quickly engulfed Europe and other nations including the USA, in what became known as the First World War or 'Great War'. Historically it has been said that the Kaiser was taking revenge for Germany losing the Franco-Prussian War in the nineteenth century.

My grandfather was immediately called up by his old regiment and eventually became a sergeant major, although his service record in 1914 described him, on two occasions, as a private with the Labour Corps in the names of Goodridge and Windebank, which must have caused some confusion in his regimental records. It was probably overlooked in the circumstances.

Nonetheless, a notice at Belfast Cathedral dated 13th August 1914 sent wishes for 'Good Luck in the name of the Lord' to the Dorsetshire Regiment. This was nine days after war was declared. The 1st Battalion of the 15th Brigade of the 5th Division of my grandfather's regiment had been stationed in Belfast and then shipped out to Le Havre in France on 16th August 1914. True to form, on the 2nd June 1915, my grandfather absented himself from a tattoo, was confined to barracks for ten days and docked twenty-one days' pay. Later that year on 12th October he overstayed his pass by one day thirty-five minutes and was admonished again. This at a time when all hell was breaking loose around him.

The army records indicate that during 1914, 1915 and 1916 my grandfather took part in the battles of the Mons and Ypres (twice). He must therefore have obtained a rise in rank to sergeant due to leading his men and bravery in battle.

In 1917 the regiment took part in the pursuit of the German Army in retreat to the Hindenburg Line. The National Roll of the Great War confirms that my grandfather also saw action on the Western Front and survived the 'retreat from Mons' and distinguished himself in other important battles, including Ypres and the Somme. During these battles he was wounded twice in action, once when a bullet went through his hand.

Following the Western Front, his battalion was shipped out to Poona and this may explain photographs of my grandfather wearing a pith helmet and army shorts.

After the Armistice of 1918, he was transferred to the reserve again and re-enlisted with the Chinese Labour Corps in the repatriation of displaced Chinese to their homeland.

Having sorted that out and the 'Windebank' alias problem, my grandfather was discharged from the army in 1920. Following this, he was eventually awarded the Mons Star and the General Service and Victory Medals.

Both of my maternal grandparents passed away in 1953. My grandmother was sixty years of age and shortly after my grandfather followed at the age of sixty-three. I have a vivid memory of the messages of their passing being delivered to our home by a telegram boy and my mother's sadness afterwards. Yet again she was shedding many tears in her losses.

Whatever happened in her life, my mother maintained a kindly disposition full of love, good humour and quiet generosity, which touched everybody she met. Luckily, she went through life in good health and her sisters were seemingly her best friends, always laughing.

Sadly, after a short illness my mother passed away in November 2003, aged eighty-one, a great loss. She gave me my life and her values which have remained in my heart forever. I bless her every day.

My father, a man of yarns

Leslie Henry William Chainey was born on 30th June 1925 at May Tree Road, Newtown, Southampton. His birth certificate recorded his father, Henry Chainey, as a merchant seaman and his mother, Elsie (formerly Sayers), as a housewife. My father's family came from decent, hard working stock.

My father preferred to be called Les and was one of seven siblings, Phyllis (the eldest), Edward (Ted), Frederick (Fred), Herbert (Bert), Mary (Herbert's twin) and Margaret (Marg).

Sadly, when my father was seven years old, his brother, Ted, died in 1932 and was followed by his other Fred in 1939. They both died of tuberculosis. These were heartbreaking losses for two young brothers, and tragic for the family as a whole. Thankfully, I have a photograph of all three brothers playing together. Each has a big smile on their face and this seems to be a family characteristic that has stayed with us forever. Certainly, my brother, Paul, and I have always seen the funny side of life!

In the 1920s and 1930s, families were trying very hard to recover their lives from the war damage. There was some employment, but workers had to get as many jobs as possible to feed their families. My grandfather managed to find work in the dockyards, but it was not certain, due to difficulties elsewhere in the country and worldwide.

Suddenly, in the USA on 24th October 1929 the Wall Street Crash began as thirteen million shares were wiped off stock. This affected American loans to countries in Europe and the world economy as a whole.

Between 1930 and 1932, with unemployment continuing to rise (it got to two million), Britain was rumoured to be heading towards bankruptcy. This led to the collapse of the Labour government in 1931, riots in many cities provoked by hunger-marchers and mutiny in the Royal Navy due to service pay cuts. A coalition government was formed, followed by a general election in October of the same year, in which the Conservatives achieved a landslide victory. However, this did not improve the employment situation and the hardships endured by the working classes continued to get worse. The situation was compounded by the following harsh winter, cuts in unemployment benefits and an unpopular means test for the 'dole'. Unemployment continued to rise to almost three million.

All of this affected my father's family badly. My grandfather lost his job and like many others had to walk the streets of Southampton in search of work. My father told me that things became so bad that on one occasion my grandfather left home and did not return until three days later, having worked the whole of that time, in fear that if he did not do so, his family would starve. Upon return to his home, my grandfather, cold, dishevelled, gaunt and hungry, in a state of near collapse and (having handed my grandmother whatever money he had earned) took to his bed and did not surface until three days later.

Eventually, when my grandfather returned to work my father would deliver, on foot, to my grandfather's workplace in the docks (a journey of about three miles each way) a billycan of home-made soup and bread prepared by my grandmother. Not only did my grandfather work in the docks, he also worked in the clay quarry pit at Witts Hill, Midanbury, Southampton, such was the pressure upon him to continue to support his family at those difficult times. Shortly before he died, my father told me that the owner of the quarry was a distant relative of the Chainey family.

One of my father's family stories was that, on the cusp of his teens, he climbed the steeple on Bitterne church. How and why I do not know. Having reached the top he couldn't get down. The local policeman and fire brigade got involved and rescued him with a stern telling off which was repeated at home. The irony of this story is that many years later this foolhardy caper stood him in good stead for his future career as a scaffolder/steeplejack.

My father told me another story involving the fire brigade when a big fire occurred on the large estate at Thornhill, near the same village. It was a very warm day in summertime. In the 1930s, Bitterne had its own part-time fire brigade drawn from the local community with its own fire pump on wheels. Not only were the brigade equipped with their own pump, but they also had helmets, fire- axes, boots and a bugle for alarms. Very smart. Unfortunately, the estate was on a hill rising up from the village.

The bugle was sounded by one of the brigade and it took a while to gather them up. Having assembled up all their gear and with the pump glistening in the summer sun, the brigade proudly started running up the hill towards the estate, with a lot of puff, sweat and effort accompanied by an audience of locals, including my father and other children, all excited by the drama.

Just as the village brigade reached the top of the hill to deal with the fire, a loud rumble of horses running fast, with bridles jingling, could be heard coming from the opposite direction, as the Southampton fire brigade loomed into view with their large horse-drawn fire engine, having attended to the fire and put it out. Slowing down, pouring sweat and not a little crestfallen, the village brigade turned around and adjourned to the nearest pub to cool down from their not inconsiderable efforts.

My father's education started at West End Infant School and then Bitterne Church of England School, as did his brothers and sisters. He admits he was not academically strong, but he was physically robust and liked all sports. He was also a strong swimmer. He could manage the three Rs but yearned for a career in the open air. It was no surprise therefore, that upon leaving school at fourteen years of age, he chose bricklaying.

Throughout his life my father was very generous and would help anybody in difficulty. I remember when my Uncle Fred (who was disabled by the war) was in dire straits, financially, and my father was the first in coming to his rescue.

By the time he left school in 1939, the drums of World War Two war were sounding in Europe and before too long conscription was on its way. This would deprive many men such as my father from being able to continue their chosen career. It was therefore inevitable that my father would answer the call to arms in one of the three services, Royal Air Force, British Army or Royal Navy. My father's family had strong connections with the sea around the Solent and the port towns of Southampton and Portsmouth.

Dorothy Bliss (nee Goodridge) as an ambulance driver, 1943

Les Chainey (middle row, fourth from left) serving in Portsmouth,
World War II

World War II - my father joined the Royal Navy

At the age of seventeen a young man was found in a bush near his parents' home in the village of Bitterne. The local policeman who found him said he was quite asleep and drunk. That young man was my father and well known to the officer. As with others he joined the Royal Navy on 2nd December 1942 to serve king and country. In order to join, he changed his year of birth to a year earlier, making him underage at the time. The country needed any capable person in the bid 'to bring down Hitler and the Nazi's' (my father's words) even if they were drunk.

According to my father's sister, Margaret, my grandmother was distraught at hearing the news of her eldest son's enlistment as a volunteer and that he was going away immediately. She reminded my father of the horrors of war, as experienced by my grandfather in the First World War, and the loss of his brother, hoping that it might be all over by the end of New Year. True to character, no amount of reasoning could dissuade my father from his course; he was going off to war and that was it.

As it turned out, my grandparents need not have worried too much because after initial training as an ordinary seaman my father was assigned to local defence duties at the naval training establishments, *HMS Victory*, *HMS Collingwood* (Portsmouth) and *HMS Selsey* (Selsey Bill nearby). This was for most of the war, save some time at sea on the aircraft carrier, *HMS Indomitable*, having risen to the rank of able seaman. As a matter of record, the establishments at Portsmouth provided the control and command centres for the D-Day landings on 6th June 1944 and other centres until the end of the war. My father was in one of the centres.

Interestingly, at my father's funeral in 2010, a man came up to me and said he knew my father on the aircraft carrier. The man himself was a Fleet Air Arm pilot.

One of the lighter stories arising from my father's time in the Navy was told to me by my Uncle Cecil, who was also in the Royal Navy. He said that he and another sailor were making their way home from Portsmouth to Southampton. They were on bicycles, having just got off their ship, when suddenly a Rolls Royce car came motoring by, with a sailor leaning out of the window, giving my uncle and his friend the V for victory sign. That sailor in the Rolls was my father who had not thought to offer a lift to my uncle. Shortly after the war, this lack of charity was redeemed when my father introduced my uncle to my mother's sister, Mary. Thus all ended well when they eventually got married.

Following his discharge on the 5th July 1946, my father returned to work in the building industry, firstly as a scaffolder and then a foreman, ending up as a steeplejack.

My father's ancestry

As mentioned, my father's parents were Elsie Chainey (nee Sayers) and Henry Chainey. According to the Census of 1911 they were born in 1895 and 1899 respectively, in Southampton, and remained there throughout their lives.

I am not sure when the family moved to Commercial Street, but it must have been during the late 1920s to early 1930s, because all the children were educated at the Church of England school in the catchment area of Bitterne. My father was taught by Miss Mist (otherwise known as 'Foggy') and Mr Mew (otherwise known as 'Pussy Mew'). When I joined the same school in 1953, Miss Mist and Mr Mew were still teaching.

The Sayers

My grandmother was one of five siblings, Ada, Hilda, Jack and William (Bill). They all lived in the same area of Bitterne, as families did in those days.

Great Uncle Jack Sayers, who never married, joined the Merchant Navy when he was young and sailed regularly on the Cunard ocean liners, such as *RM Queen Mary* and *Queen Elizabeth* travelling between Southampton and New York and on other such ships worldwide. He was extremely jolly and full of interesting stories about far away places he had visited and the people he had seen, including film stars coming across the Atlantic Sea.

He was quite deaf and when I asked my father how he lost his hearing, he said it was as a result of taking on the American longshoremen in bare-knuckle fights to earn extra money, having docked at New York. Not only did he enjoy his work (which kept him away from home for long periods, hence his bachelor status), he also took part as a volunteer seaman in the rescue of the British Expeditionary Force from of Dunkirk in 1940.Unfortunately, his ship was sunk by the Germans, but luckily he was rescued by another vessel and made it safely back home.

Always the life and soul of a party, Uncle Jack, after a good dose of stout and whisky, would lighten up family gatherings, particularly at Christmas time, with laughter and songs. He would be joined by my Irish Uncle Kevin (husband to my father's sister, Aunt Mary) and my father jigging along with the sailor's hornpipe.

The pugilist in Uncle Jack may have derived from an earlier ancestor named Tom Sayers, who in the mid-to-late nineteenth century was the bare-knuckle boxing champion of England and the idol of the dandies, who would place large bets upon him to win fights. Such was his fame that he was as revered a sports star as those of today. Having out-boxed all contestants within his weight, Sayers would take on all-comers above that weight until, with great success, he ran out of any further opponents.

Famously, and having looked further afield, a fight was arranged with John Heenan, the American champion, at Farnborough, Hampshire on 17th April 1860. At five foot eight inches, Tom Sayers conceded forty pounds in weight and five inches in height. Early on in the fight he broke his arm and continued using his good arm. After two hours the fight was broken up by the police. Shortly after this, Tom Sayers decided to retire from boxing. The public, in gratitude, raised £3000 to ensure a comfortable retirement for their courageous champion. Troubled by tuberculosis and diabetes, Tom Sayers died on 8th November 1865, aged only thirty-nine, and was buried at Highgate Cemetery together with his dog, Lion. His funeral cortege in London was attended by ten thousand people. I have in my possession a porcelain a figurine of the Sayers/Heenan fight and some portraits of him. Tom Sayers was married with three children. There is a strong resemblance between him and my father.

Back to my grandmother, my young brother and I wondered why she always put her hat on, together with a very long and vicious looking hat-pin, when leaving the house. In fact, all her sisters would do the same. I was always baffled because they would keep their hats on throughout afternoon tea, whilst the men had to take theirs off. This was made all the more interesting thinking that the hat-pins might have punctured grandmother's head.

A Brazilian Footballer named 'Little Bird'

Not having a TV and being avid football fans, on FA Cup Final days my brother and I would visit Great Uncle's Bill's house to watch the game with our father, because no one else in the immediate family had a television. This was in the early 1950s. In fact we also watched Brazil playing England and all of us were mesmerised by two Brazilian players, named Pele and Garrincha, otherwise known as 'Little Bird', who would become one of my football idol in the 1950s.

Note: As to my maternal grandmother's ancestry I know little of this, save that my father told me his grandmother was named Sarah James. From the Census for Hampshire up to 1911, I could only trace a Sarah James from Stoneham in 1846.

Having researched for my father's family tree I only discovered that my great grandfather was Francis William Chainey, born in 1861 in Southampton, who was married to Eliza Jane Bundy. Unfortunately, I have no further details. I do know that my grandfather, Henry Chainey was one of eight children, namely himself, Frank, Alice, Charles, Lucy, Fred, Thomas and Elizabeth. The Census for Hampshire from the mid nineteenth century up to 1911 does record a Charles Claxton Chainey born in 1864 and that is as far as I can take this aspect of the ancestry on my grandfather's side. That said, my father told me that Charles (my great uncle) was very dapper in that he wore a bowler hat, white shirt and tie and spats, and carried a cane. He was stern and did not tolerate fools.

My father did tell me that one of his ancestors was a foundling (a new-born baby usually left outside a workhouse) and taken into care, but he could say no more. I can find no other trace of this.

The Great War 1914 – 1918

However, I do know as a matter of fact in the National Roll of the Great War, my grandfather, Henry, joined the British Army Machine-Gun Corps in April 1917 and, following a short training as a gunner, was sent to the Western Front. In this theatre of war it is recorded that he took part in heavy fighting in a number of sectors and fought in many important engagements right up to the end of the war. He was demobilised in January 1919 and was awarded the General Service and Victory medals. It is perhaps enlightening to record that when an attack by the enemy across no man's land was attempted, the gunners of the MGC would fire obliquely across the front of advancing troops, thereby creating a deadly hail of bullets, which resulted in the attack coming to a disastrous and very tragic halt. Henry was a very quiet man and on winter nights he would sit near the fire to watch the red and yellow flames rising up. He was a real warrior and hero fighting for his king and country.

My Great-Uncle Frederick (Henry's brother) had enlisted with the 15th Hampshire Regiment in September 1916 and was also posted to the Western Front where he, like his brother, fought in a number of sectors, including the battles of the Somme and the Aisne. He was severely wounded on two occasions in action. Tragically, Fred was killed in action at Menin on the 14th October 1918, less than one month before the war came to an end. His brother, Henry, was beside him and survived. Frederick was also a great warrior and hero fighting for king and country and received the General Service and Victory medals.

Both my grandfather and my great uncle are recorded to have been living at Clarence Street, Southampton when they enlisted in the Army. Frederick's name appears on the Cenotaph at Southampton. Recently my cousin, Mrs Lin Callaway, visited with her husband, Steve, the military grave of Frederick at Menin on the hundredth anniversary of the armistice of the Great War in 1918.

Christmas came and went and the Great War (as it came to be known) rumbled on into 1915. Germany had invaded Belgium just before 4th August 1914 and Britain declared war on Germany to protect the neutrality of Belgium following the Treaty of London 1839. The German Army then invaded France (their intended goal at the outset) by launching vicious, sustained and extensive bombardments, reducing the countryside of both countries to a quagmire and resulting in the stalemate of the various armies in trench warfare. It was to go on for four years. At the end of hostilities, the nation hoped 'that was the war to end all wars'.

My grandfather never talked about the war. I noticed that on many occasions he would sit in his armchair staring at the flames in his fireplace lost in his thoughts never to be disturbed. As I grew up I often wondered if within those thoughts were the painful memories of what he endured and of those people he knew would never come back. Much later, I was informed that my grandfather was gassed at the battle of Ypres and wounded at the battle of the Somme. Despite that, he smoked full strength Senior Service cigarettes without 'spats on' throughout his life.

As time went by my grandmother suffered badly with arthritis, eventually resulting in two hip replacements. She spent her later years in a wheelchair. In the spirit of a Chainey, she kept her humour. I loved going to my grandparents' every week because there was warmth, laughter and comfort.

Sadly, my grandfather died in the summer of 1972. My grandmother never overcame her loss and died in the following December. On the day of her death, my brother and I visited our granny in hospital and in the evening she passed away. The nurse who was with her told us that when she died her arms were outstretched as if in some form of a divine welcoming. Needless to say, my grandparents were sadly missed by all of our families and are still thought of by those of us who had known them very dearly. I was very bereft of their losses.

Their son, my father, passed away in March 2010. In his later days and after the passing of my mother he became a bit of a jolly raconteur, regaling the family with one tale after another, some of which were hilarious in the extreme. For the times of laughter he gave us, he will always be remembered with love.

Part 3
A not so 'brief encounter' and a post-war wedding with a family home for sixty years

Early years

In1946 Britain was broke and the people were subjected to austere measures, such as severe rationing, including bread, for the first time in history. The Ministry of Food even circulated a recipe for squirrel pie! Conscription was still in force and vast numbers of the armed forces were gradually returning home from service abroad and the various war zones. Nationally, a massive clearing up operation was put in hand with a view to rebuilding those areas devastated by enemy action. Southampton town centre was virtually wiped out by aggressive bombing and it would take some time to complete the reconstruction of the damaged areas, some of which would, in the meantime, become playgrounds for children including me and my brother.

That same year a young man was cycling along Northam Bridge, Southampton on his way home after a day's work, when he spotted a young lady trying to deal with a punctured tyre on her bicycle. In a gesture of old-fashioned chivalry, the young man helped the young lady to mend her tyre and sent her on her way. This petite drama was played out by my mother and father. Contrary to the film showing in cinemas at that time, this was not to become a brief encounter because my father found out where my mother worked in her cake shop.

Following a period of courtship, my parents were married in a civil ceremony on 26th April, 1947. The witnesses were my mother's eldest brother, Cecil Goodridge, and my father's uncle, Bill Sayers.

Up until petrol rationing came to an end in May 1950 and food rationing in July 1954, times were very difficult for young families. Accordingly, my father, who was a keen gardener, set about growing food for our family.

The garden at our new home was large enough to sow a sustainable crop of vegetables of all descriptions, as well as numerous fruit bushes and apple and pear trees. In addition, my father created flower beds and hedgerows at the front and back of the house.

As time rolled by, the products my father's endeavours matured so much that each year we had a bountiful harvest of good wholesome home grown food, helped along by a generous heap of steaming pig manure dumped in our garden every summer. At that time of year, my mother had to wait until the dung was deeply dug into the ground before hanging out the washing.

In order to complement his stock for the family my father acquired two allotments nearby. By that time gardening had become his hobby, which he enjoyed together with his brother, Bert, and other gardeners.

In consequence of all of this, the preparation of food at home was a family affair at a time when there was no such thing as ready-made meals. My brother and I would on the weekends gather in the fruit, top and tail gooseberries and blackcurrants, shuck peas and broad beans, clean potatoes, carrots, swede and turnips (to mention just a few) whilst mother, with her baking skills, set about the preparation and cooking of our meals, including the baking of delicious fruit pies and cakes. In fact, with hindsight, we were from the beginning, brought up on organic food before it ever became popular as a product today.

In those days, mealtimes were a very important time for the family to get together and discuss what we had done in the day and what we would be doing the next day. In our house there was always much laughter and interest between all of us as we were speaking. In a gesture of respect to our parents we would ask to leave the dining table when we had eaten our meal, particularly on Sunday lunch time.

As to home comforts, there was initially no central heating in our home, so we were heated by an open fire in the lounge with a back-boiler to warm the next door dining room via a metal panel drawing heat from the fire. There was no washing machine but a copper tub had been installed in the kitchen to wash all our clothes, bed linen and other such items, which were dried on a washing line outdoors and indoors with the use of a mangle. My brother and I assisted mother in using the mangle when large items such as sheets were fed into it. On occasions when it was very windy, the washing line would snap and sheets, pillow cases and clothes would fly everywhere until we could retrieve them. My brother and I thought that was fun, whilst our mother had to count the cost of having to wash some items again. At the end of the 1950s, we still had no TV or telephone. When I was eight years old, I joined the PDSA 'Busy Bees', working in the rescue of smaller animals, as a junior.

The winters at home were challenging to the extent that on cold nights the bedrooms would be, quite literally, freezing. In consequence, at bedtime, pyjamas, slippers, dressing-gowns, a hot cup of cocoa or Horlicks and a hot water bottle were imperative. In the mornings our windows were a kaleidoscope of wonderful patterns created by Jack Frost as my father said! The sound of planes flying into Eastleigh airport during the night is one I have carried with me throughout my life. The planes of the day were Dragon Rapide bi-planes, Dakotas and large Silver City Carriers all flying over Eastleigh day and night.

In the morning we were always woken by our father listening to the BBC shipping forecasts, 'Cromarty, Forth, Dogger, Fair Isle, fresh to strong gales, south to southwest, visibility poor' etcetera. I also used to hear with glee the horns of ships when the Docks were surrounded by great mists blown from the sea in, mainly in wintertime.

After my father had gone to work, breakfast was served up by our mother, before we went to school. This usually consisted of cereals such as Weetabix, Shredded Wheat or Puffed Wheat and porridge. My parents regarded breakfast to be the most important meal of the day and this is something I have carried throughout my life. On Sundays we usually had a good English lunch of roast meat and potatoes, home grown vegetables, Yorkshire Pudding and gravy, rounded off with mother's home-made cakes, pies, puddings, you name it, and a great dollop of custard.

From left, Paul, Leslie, Dorothy and Peter, 1959

A very merry Christmas

I was always very excited at Christmas time, not only at home but at my school where the story of the three kings and the coming of Jesus always engrossed me as a wonderful story. To this day, I still celebrate the festive season with my family, relatives and others around me. Our Sunday school always gave us a good Christmas party in their hall.

In the 1950s, my father had to work right up to the end of Christmas Eve when he would be paid his wages. My mother would then rush into town by bus to meet him and to do last minute shopping, having just been given my father's money. That was very difficult, but my mother was determined that we would have a good festive holiday, always.

Christmas day lunch was always eaten at home in the usual way with all the trimmings, although my father could not eat fowl, so we had meats. My mother always made her own Christmas pudding, mince pies and Christmas cake which would be complemented by a traditional Tunis cake (always a family favourite). On Boxing Day, we would have bubble-and-squeak, hams and father's home pickled onions in jars which he gave to the whole family.

We would then traditionally have a family party with one or other of our relatives. If there was a local FC football game in the afternoon on a Sunday, the men would go to the Dell Football Stadium to watch Southampton play. On return of the men, in the early evening, we would all play games like apple in a bucket and blind man's lap, followed with singing and dancing from everybody including children. Merriment and friendship galore.

Peter, front row, middle, pixie, 1958

When he was able to, my father took Paul and I to watch the Saints. We were always in the stands where we had a good view of the game. On cold, wet and sometimes misty winter days we were suitably wrapped up in warm clothes, although I noted that once amongst the crowd we could take comfort from the numerous warm bodies around us. My mother never went with us. Paul and I have been fans of the team throughout our lives.

My football idols in the fifties were Duncan Edwards of Manchester United, Stanley Matthews of Blackpool and Tom Finney of Preston North End. I was very upset when Duncan Edwards lost his life in the Manchester football team plane crash at Munich in 1958. The news of that tragic event was given to our teacher in the afternoon at school. The head teacher closed the school down and sent us home early, as a gesture of respect. I still remember that day very clearly.

I remember our Christmas presents usually consisted of a cowboy, Red Indian or knight's outfit, annuals or other books such as an encyclopaedia, a Dinky toy, a tin of Swift Toffees and new slippers. On one occasion, Paul woke up at about four a.m. on Christmas Day, put on his new cowboy outfit with gun, holster and hat then climbed back into bed and fell asleep. Come the morning his hat was all crumpled up, much to the amusement (or disappointment) of our parents. I still have some of those items.

Through my childhood and right up to my teens, I amassed a considerable number of toys and Airfix model aeroplanes which kept me fully occupied and amused as any young boy would be. I particularly enjoyed the cowboy and Indian Swoppet toys and zoo animals, produced by Britains, the toy makers. They were very popular and sold out regularly. I also collected a large number of American cars manufactured by Corgi by way of furthering my interest in the USA. Whatever happened to all of these I do not know, although I suspect they were given to other young members of the family when I left home.

As the New Year unfolded, we looked forward to the snow and having snowball fights with other friends on the estate. We used tea trays for toboggan racing down the snowy slopes and built numerous snowmen, all of which kept us outdoors for hours, returning home at the end of the day, wet and cold, but wholly satisfied with the fun we had. The harshest winter I can remember occurred in 1963, when snow was still on the ground right up to April.

My mother: a fine cook, garment knitter and homemaker

My mother was an excellent cook and during the winter she would prepare and serve up such traditional English food as beef or lamb stew with dumplings and root vegetables, Lancashire hot pot, steak and kidney pie, ham and split pea soup, as well as the traditional Sunday roast. These were all accompanied by desserts such as apple or rhubarb pie, jam roly-poly, spotted dick, treacle tart and syrup pudding. In addition, my mother would also prepare and bake sponges, such as Victoria jam, gooseberry, blackcurrant and coconut chocolate and coffee. The list was not exhaustive as my mother would also conjure up delicious meals from the leftovers of the weekend joint.

As well as cooking, my mother enjoyed knitting and kept us all well supplied with jumpers, cardigans and pullovers, together with complementary headgear such as woollen pompom hats and balaclava helmets. Overall our parents made our childhoods safe, warm, loved and cared for with good values.

As I grew older, my mother went to work in the kitchen at Thornhill School. This enabled her, after a while, to attend an external cookery course, upon completion of which she rose quickly to the position of assistant cook. This was the only fulltime job my mother ever had during my lifetime, although to supplement the household income, she would work temporarily at Woolworths in the weeks before Christmas.

For pleasure, she went to the cinema six times to see *Gone with the Wind* (first time in 1940) and five times to *The Sound of Music*, mostly with her sisters or friends and once with me. Later I took four different girls, at their begging, to see *The Sound of Music* in one year. It was very popular at the time and I liked the music.

Although he was happy in his work in the sixties, my father started to look elsewhere and considered two alternative job opportunities, mainly to try and secure his future domestically and financially. One was with a construction company in South Africa and the other was as a prison officer, based at Dartmoor. After much consideration neither job was taken for two reasons, so far as I recall. The first was that both mother and father were happily settled with Paul and I in our current home at a critical time in our schooling and the upheaval would have been very unsettling. The second was that they were unhappy about moving so far away from their families and friends, to whom they were very close.

In the event, my father was promoted to foreman in his scaffolding job which increased his ability to earn more money in secure employment. In fact, his job elevated him to the status of a steeplejack, working on high-rise jobs such as the Severn Bridge, St. Paul's Cathedral and two chimney stacks at Fawley Oil Refinery. It was on the refinery job that my father had a near fatal accident in the 1950s. He was ascending one of the stacks in a cradle with another worker. When they reached a height of almost one hundred feet, their cradle was rocked by a gust of wind from the Solent, causing my father to be tipped out of his cradle. This was at a time of no proper safety gear or hard hats. As he fell, my father hit a heavy duty iron mesh protruding from the unfinished stack, which slowed his fall, and was caught by a tarpaulin held out by other quick-thinking workmen alerted to this impending disaster. Luckily my father suffered only a fractured shinbone, some bruises and shock. He quickly recovered and returned to work as soon as he could, because his employer did not make any sickness payments during his absence.

Life Boy and Scout

When I was nine years old I joined the Life Boys, the junior section of the Boys' Brigade. The uniform consisted of a sailor's hat, knitted fisherman's jumper, shorts and socks, all navy blue, with black shoes. The tops of the socks were folded over and red tabs would show from under the fold at my knees. Meetings took place in the church hall, Pound Street, Bitterne. The hat was worn tilted to the right of the head. A lanyard completed the outfit. The Boys' Brigade was founded in 1883 and remains a Christian Youth Organisation. Its motto is 'Sure and Steadfast'. I recall that being a Life Boy entailed drill and activities with Christian values including promotion of obedience, reverence, discipline and self-respect. The Life Boys' badge was awarded after two years' service. I have never been frightened of the sea or going on a boat.

After two years, my focus was on joining the Boy Scouts Organisation, where I had a number of friends. It is worth noting that Robert Baden-Powell, founder of the Scout movement, was made a Vice-President of the Boys Brigade in the early 1900s.

In 1908 Baden-Powell published his book, *Scouting for Boys*. It was loosely based upon military scouting and activities learnt in the Boer War. The book contained what amounted to an informal educational programme emphasising outdoor activities such as camping, woodcraft, hiking, backpacking, sports and orienteering. This was in stark contrast to the Life Boys and appealed to my growing nature.

In 1959 at the age eleven, I joined the 21st Itchen Scout Troop. Meetings took place in a corrugated tin hut in Hadley Road, Bitterne. We were eighteen strong with two scoutmasters called 'skips'. I was in Eagle patrol. I had two friends in the troop, including Derek Burke (who, when he completed his education went to work in Southampton docks, becoming a labour councillor and mayor of Southampton twice).

I enjoyed scouting and swearing allegiance to the queen and God at meetings. My focus was on earning my badges (which I did) and involving myself in as many activities as possible, preferably outdoors. This became possible when we camped in the New Forest. One of the most challenging activities was orienteering at night time using night compasses. We were divided into squads of three and delivered by jeep to the middle of the forest. Using the stars as direction finders along with the compasses we would plot a course back to camp. Some got lost and took a little time to return, but nobody got lost for good. In fact, searching for the errant squad was an interesting challenge in itself.

Camping was great fun. Upon arrival we would raise the Union Jack, sometimes with a bugler. We would then set up tents and make ready our fires, including gathering tinder and lighting it, using two sticks, in readiness for our meals. One of my favourites was cooking sausages and beans which I was happy to prepare with our skip on the open fire, around which we would all congregate and then sing the *ging-gang-goolly-whatsit* song and other songs, such as *On the crest of a wave*, to round off the day. On many an occasion, I would marvel at the stars, laid on my back in the warm night air, counting the constellations and identifying particular groups of stars to enable me to obtain my astrology badge.

On one winter's day we visited Avon Tyrell Activities Centre in the Forest for an early morning football competition involving the Girl Guides, in mixed teams. Some of the guides still had their pyjamas on under their kit to keep warm. I cannot remember who won, but I do recall the post-match hot showers (not with the Guides I hasten to add) followed by a breakfast of 'gruel' and toast, washed down with piping hot cups of tea.

Another enjoyable event with Scouting was bob-a-job week, normally around Easter, during which, for a shilling (five pence), we would offer to carry out tasks for householders, in part to know the community. This might entail cutting the lawn, assisting with shopping, washing cars or cleaning windows, to name but a few. I was caught out on one occasion by an elderly couple who asked me to clean their complete set of silver cutlery using a cleaning agent in powder form. It took me virtually all day and I gratefully accepted the solitary shilling paid for this tortuous task. Goodness knows what would have happened if any item had been unacceptable to them.

I never learnt to play a musical instrument well enough to join the Scout band, but marching behind the band at carnivals and other celebrations such as Armistice Day was always a proud moment and gave me a good idea of singing for the future.

The Scout gatherings at Brownsea Island, Poole, where the first Scout camp was erected in 1907 by Baden-Powell, and the Ralph Reader Gang Show, have been seminal events, attracting scouts from around the world in a sharing of their common aims and enjoyment, without any boundary. It is a testimony to the Scout movement that is still going after one hundred years, enabling young people to continue developing into rounded and responsible human beings for the benefit of others.

During the 1950s, our summer holidays were normally daily outings by coach or train to places such as London, Bournemouth, Swanage, Portsmouth, Kew Gardens, Bristol Zoo, and Windsor. I especially looked forward to visiting the Natural History and other museums in London which enabled us also to watch the changing of the guard at Buckingham Palace. On one occasion, we visited Hampton Court and by chance met Lady Baden-Powell, who was living in one of the grace and favour homes within the palace.

We also shared holidays with my father's family and I remember one particular warm sunny day we took a trip to Swanage on the Bournemouth Belle steam train. It was a Sunday and my grandparents were dressed in their finery, which in the case of my grandfather consisted of his full three piece suit and cloth cap. His only contribution to relieving his discomfort, in the heat of the day, was the removal of his shoes and socks and the rolling up of his trousers to his ankles. My grandmother, as usual, wore her hat all day. They made a wonderful picture as they dozed in their deckchairs and we together with our cousins built sandcastles around them.

There was a further occasion when our parents took Paul and I to the Isle of Wight. Again it was a hot summer's day and we travelled on the IOW paddle steamer, a wonderful experience in itself. However, during the crossing of the Solent the boat started to spew smuts of soot from its funnel, which rained down on the passengers. My father immediately sprang into action by making cocked hats with the pages from his newspaper and handing them around to all and sundry. His resourcefulness received a well-deserved round of applause.

Over the course of time, many changes were made, inevitably, to the village of Bitterne. In the mid-1950s numerous cottages and shops were demolished to make way for the building of two large stores, Fine Fare and Woolworths. This introduced the novelty of shopping in a supermarket, which became very popular and ushered in the concept of one-stop shopping. Towards the end of the decade, the Ritz Cinema gave way to a bowling alley. These developments resulted in the loss of many traders whose shops had served the community for decades, in some cases having been passed down through generations of the same family.

Eventually, the hammer blow was delivered, when in 1981, the Bitterne bypass was built and the village was converted into a pedestrian shopping precinct, to be taken over by a number of soulless banks, building societies and estate agents, with the concomitant loss of the character and soul of the community.

Despite these changes, the Red Lion was salvaged and serves to this day as a reminder of more sedate times, long gone but not forgotten, thanks to the committed descendants of families who helped to create and support the very informative and thriving Bitterne History Society for future generations.

Part 4
The tragic loss of my beloved brother and soul mate

The tragic loss of my beloved brother and soul mate

On Sunday the 31st May 1992 my dear brother, Paul, died, having been struck down at work the day before by a fatal aneurysm on his brain. His death was so sudden and crushing I was numb and could not believe what I had heard. He was only forty-two years age and at the top of his lifetime.

The shock of his death was unbearable and resonant with all those close to him. The immediate family, particularly my dear mother, father, sister, his daughter, Gabrielle, and Diana, his second wife, were devastated at the inexplicable loss of such a vibrant and gifted character. The effects of this tragedy are still with us all.

The Thursday before that fateful weekend, I had spoken with Paul who was in good spirits and looking forward to going out for an Indian meal with his wife, Diana, and their close friends, Malcolm and Sue, the following Saturday. On that Saturday I had arranged to see Nigel Kennedy, the popular violinist, performing Vivaldi's *Four Seasons* at Winchester Cathedral. Fate ordained that this was not to happen.

This tragedy started to unfold when on 30th May I received a very distressing telephone call from Diana, who told me that Paul had gone to work that morning in Portsmouth with a blinding headache. Apparently, at about eight-thirty a.m., Paul collapsed at his employer's premises and was found, unconscious, by a colleague. Paul was rushed by ambulance to the Queen Alexandra Hospital where, following examination he was placed on a life-support machine.

I was outside in the garden when my mother telephoned my (then) girlfriend, Lizzie, at nine-fifteen a.m. to tell me that Paul had been taken to hospital and that his condition was very serious. Lizzie and I stopped what we were doing and immediately drove to Southampton General Hospital, neurological unit, where my mother had been told he would be. At the unit we were told by a doctor that they had been waiting for Paul to be delivered by ambulance from Queen Alexandra Hospital,

Portsmouth, but that Paul's condition had deteriorated to the extent that he would not now be transferred to Southampton.

Lizzie and I feared the worst and quickly made our way to the Queen Alexandra Hospital. Upon arriving in the intensive care unit, we saw Paul unconscious and wired up to the life support machine. My parents and Diana were there in a very distressed state. I held Paul's hand but there was no response from him. We decided to stay with Paul on the ward in the vain hope that there might be some improvement in his condition. As the day moved on and the doctors continued to monitor the position, our hopes began to fade. Later in the day we were called to an adjoining room where we had a meeting with the two doctors in charge of Paul.

We were told that Paul's condition was not going to change and that difficult decisions had to be made in the light of this. Neither Diana nor my parents could bring themselves to make the unbearable decision to turn off his life support machine. After further discussions amongst us including the doctors, and having been assured that clinically there was no hope of Paul's recovery, I reluctantly and tearfully made the agonising decision for his life support machine to be switched off. He was certified dead the following day.

On that Sunday, when collecting some of Paul's possessions, I was told by one of the doctors that Paul's heart continued beating for one hour after the life support machine had been switched off. We were all stunned and for quite a time could not take in the loss of the wonderful and loveable man named Paul.

At his funeral, I and some of Paul's friends carried his coffin into the chapel to the tune of *We are the champions* sung by his favourite pop band, Queen. During the service, I delivered a eulogy on the themes of happiness, love, his family, friends and art, at which Paul excelled. There were many people in attendance and at the wake, at Paul and Diana's home, there was nothing but praise for him and his laughter in remembrance of his vital personality.

Paul's ashes were buried at Bitterne Church cemetery and I continue to visit his grave regularly. He will be with me in my heart and soul forever and every day I say a little prayer to my heavenly brother, Paul.

So who was Paul to me?

First and foremost he was my younger brother, best friend and soul mate. He was very close to me, having been born twenty months after me. Such a short age difference between us guaranteed a strong and loving togetherness throughout our lives. He was a star who twinkled all the time. His delightful daughter, Gabrielle, has grown up in the image of her father.

There is an early photograph of Paul taken at our coronation street party. He had copper coloured hair and freckles, which he disliked with a vengeance and reacted to angrily if any comment was made about it. This was not helped when our father addressed Paul as 'Ginger', to which he would sneer. Fortunately, as he grew into his teens his colouring changed to light auburn hair and his freckles faded away.

Paul was in some ways a complex and very enigmatic character. In our earlier years we were inseparable and very supportive of each other. It was only when our secondary educations beckoned that our paths went in separate directions, me to Merry Oak and Paul to Moorhill, for our schooling. This did not blemish in any way our close relationship, even though we had different interests and circles of friends. I can honestly say that we were a real band of brothers.

In addition to this, I can safely say that to some extent Paul was my rudder through life on many occasions. We could confide in each other in the difficult times in our lives, not so much to provide a solution, but simply to lend a sympathetic ear and talk through any problem, or share the most intimate concerns in our lives, particularly as we grew older. For example, Paul proudly divulged to me his own ideas as to how to give girls 'maximum pleasure', a topic about which we both had our own ideas, especially when it came to intimacy. I would listen to his pearls of wisdom with bemusement, bearing in mind that he was younger than me. In short, we could give each other direction and did so.

There were also a number of times when Paul would bottle up something that was really bothering him. This naturally concerned my mother who said she could talk to me, I assume because I was the older brother with a different temperament, but never to Paul, for fear of receiving a sharp and very negative response. This is not to say that there was no communication between them, but my mother had to carefully seize the moment when she felt comfortable approaching her second son.

I remember one occasion in our teens when mother told me that she thought Paul had a 'love-bite' on his neck and she was concerned that he might get some girl into trouble. I assured my mother that this was unlikely, knowing Paul as I did, and not to worry about it. I also offered to talk to Paul (which I did) and his response was typical and along the lines of, "It doesn't bother me, so why should it bother anybody else." Nothing more came of it, save that eventually he married the girl concerned (his first wife, Diana).

Paul also had a wicked sense of humour. On one occasion, when we went to the Southampton Show in the summer of 1967, there was a horticulture tent, displaying cacti on a table. On seeing this, Paul quickly quipped, "Look Pete, nobulus erecti," pointing to a table full of phallic-shaped cacti of all sizes. He purchased three different sizes and kept them on the windowsill in his bedroom.

After leaving junior school, Paul went to Moorhill Secondary School which was built in the early sixties on the Harefield estate (it is now known as Woodlands Community College). It was co-educational and before long Paul had acquired a large number of friends, male and female, being a real magnet.

After some time, Paul and his coterie of friends had one thing in common; they took up smoking (Paul was fourteen years old at the time). At the end of the school day, Paul and his friends would have a whip round of money and spend the proceeds on a packet or two of five Woodbines, decanting to the nearest copse for the rest of the afternoon. My parents (who did not smoke) did not become aware of this until my father, returning home from work early one day, saw Paul and two of his chums walking along Somerset Avenue, still in school uniform, nonchalantly puffing away like actors with cigarettes in their mouths. Words were exchanged when Paul got home, but he continued smoking for the rest of his life, albeit not at home until he was sixteen. As a matter of fact, I dabbled with smoking when I was sixteen but I never took to it and ended up a non-smoker. Incidentally, Paul's first attempt at smoking was at home with a rolled up piece of newspaper which he set alight from the fire in the front room, inhaled and almost choked, without a thought that he could burn down our home. He was about ten.

During our teens Paul and I would have differences of opinion sometimes resulting in us having a bit of a tussle which was occasionally broken up by either our mother or father. There were times when we resorted to boxing or wrestling in our lounge with the encouragement of our father, as a means of releasing tensions between us. It was all in fun really.

On one occasion at home when he was thireen, Paul called me a cunt in front of mother, who in a state of apoplexy told him to never use that kind of language in front her again. Being Paul he shrugged his shoulders, but never repeated this in front of my parents again. Swearing in our house was strictly forbidden and Paul was becoming a man very quickly.

As time went on Paul did well at school and was particularly talented in art, which he went on to achieve at GCE grade A and then repeated at A-level in his exams. He was also good at sports, specially football, resulting in him being placed into many sports at school events. He finished his schooling in 1966.

My brother, Paul (left) on his wedding day, 1971

Paul's career

Paul's first job, at the age of sixteen, was as a clerk with Camper & Nicholson, shipbuilders in Southampton docks for a short while. He decided that this was not for him and he quickly got a job as a cartographer in the Ordnance Survey, Southampton (where he quickly gained excellent drawing skills). The cartographer's office was in London Road, Southampton in an old army barrack with underground jails. The Ordnance Survey also had an office for mapping and photography on the outskirts of Southampton.

Interestingly, the old jails had been turned into the staff club, providing alcohol and modern pop music. It was there that Paul made many friendships in no time at all. After a while, Paul was taking me to the club for a good night out, staying for the evening or going out to other clubs in town. It was at this time I saw Paul taking stimulants with some of his colleagues.

After taking the decision to further his career, Paul took evening classes at the local school of art to try and qualify as a commercial artist. Having qualified in his chosen field, Paul got a position with the well-known printers, Sir Joseph Causton and Sons Limited, Eastleigh as a full-time commercial artist.

Eventually, Paul was doing the artwork on magazines such as *House and Home*, *Vanity Fair*, *Harpers* and *The Lady* (to name but a few), occasionally attending their publishing houses at London and elsewhere to discuss the artwork required on a particular cover, pending printing and distribution.

Paul also had the dubious, but fun, pleasure of working on other magazines such as *Playboy*, 'touching up the pubes' (so he told me). When I reached the age of forty, Paul sent me a greetings card, produced by him, from *Playboy*, with a tantalising print of two gorgeous ladies with cheeky smiles

The artwork, printing and distribution of such popular titles was a skilful and work-intensive exercise, resulting in Paul working long hours, often through the night, due to the tight time scale for next day delivery to the shelves of distributors. For this he was handsomely rewarded and it enabled him to move forward in his life in a number of directions working in the world of art.

In September 1971, Paul married his first wife, Diana, and they moved to Calmore, near Totton and the New Forest. They then moved to Rownhams, Southampton and their daughter, Gabrielle, was born in 1979, making me an uncle. She was their only child. Sadly, their marriage did not last. Thankfully, I am still in contact with Gabby and her two children.

Following his divorce, after some time, Paul met and married his second wife, also named Diana, in 1985. She had three boys from her first marriage.

Throughout the whole of this period Paul and I kept in close contact. We would meet regularly to attend Saints' football matches and to play squash or billiards. We would go to the pub weekly, drinking Guinness, chased down with an Irish whisky. Our favourite drinking holes were the Eclipse Inn and the Old Vyne, both in The Square, Winchester.

The breakup of Paul's first marriage was taken badly by him. Even more distressing was the fact that his wife took Gabrielle to live with her in Shropshire, at the other end of the country. Whether this was intentional I do not know, but it took its toll on Paul in having to travel so far to see his daughter. It was painful to witness Paul's distress, but our close ties and his own fortitude enabled him to work his way through it, assisted by a few glasses of whisky shared together, until eventually he found love again with his second wife.

When Paul sold the matrimonial home from his first marriage he stayed at my house in Shirley, Southampton which accommodated not only him but two other housemates, both females, who got along very well. There was, however, an extraordinary incident at the property when Paul was woken one night to find two police officers in the hallway holding a third man, who had been in the process of burgling the house. Neither Paul nor his housemates were aware of anything going on!

Apparently a neighbour had spotted the burglar climbing through a back window and coming out with my hi-fi unit!

Following Paul's second marriage, life settled down and we were able to go out together with our wives for an evening meal, usually at an Indian restaurant, and entertain each other with dinner parties on a regular basis. Paul was an avid fan of the TV comedies, *Monty Python* and *Fawlty Towers*, and we would occasionally watch these to round off the evening, well-oiled and certainly well-entertained. These times were good for Paul.

At the beginning of the 1990s I noticed a significant change in Paul. He looked very tired and exhausted and his intake of whisky had increased. Talking with him about this, he confided that his workload had increased and his constant trips to see Gabrielle were becoming more and more difficult. Although Paul took comfort from being able to discuss this with me, the pressures upon him continued to grow.

Eventually, sometime early in 1992, I received a telephone call one morning from his wife, Diana, expressing her concerns about Paul's drinking. I made some excuse for visiting him at home the same morning and when Paul saw me he enquired quite brusquely what I was doing there. I noticed a glass of whisky and ashtray full of cigarette stubs on his kitchen table. We had a chat and he expressed concern that he might be made redundant from his job.

Shortly after that, I met Paul one evening for our regular meal and drink at his local pub, the Master Builder at West End. He was quite emotional and said that he feared his marriage was failing. We discussed this at some length saying that it would be potentially disastrous, financially, if his second marriage broke down. I went through this with Paul, saying that I would give him as much help as I could and to contact me by telephone night or day.

The next time I saw Paul was at the eighteenth birthday party of my youngest daughter, Anna, at my house. He looked drawn, pasty and very taut. As there were other people present, including his wife, I had little opportunity to have a discussion with him. However, I made telephone contact with Paul shortly after and made arrangements to meet up. That was the last time I saw Paul and within two weeks he was dead. My grief was heartbreaking and I pray to him every day.

With Paul's loss, a very bright light had gone out, leaving us with cherished memories of his laughter and a unique presence in our lives. He really was a one-off, loved immensely and well liked.

Shortly after Paul's funeral, my wife, Lizzie, and I, together with other members of the family including my parents, attended a party at Anna's home, at which Paul's widow, Diana, was accompanied by a man introduced to us as 'a very old friend'. My grieving father suggested, in no uncertain terms, that the presence of this unknown 'friend' was inappropriate so soon after Paul's death, whereupon Diana and her 'friend' departed. Whether or not my father's outburst was warranted is neither here nor there given the circumstances. The fact is that we never heard from Diana again.

PART 5
My school education — 1953 – 1964

Roll on

My education started some time before I went to school. At home I was surrounded by numerous books chosen by me, bought, borrowed or gifted, to pore over through my childhood.

Additionally, my parents subscribed to a number of book clubs and we as a family joined the local library, which at that time was situated at Bitterne Manor. As well as taking home two books each, my brother and I would also scan the books in the library whilst we waited for our parents to choose theirs.

I quickly became an avid reader right up to and at bed-time, regularly having one or two books on the go at the same time. In consequence, when I started school I was very literate and found reading, writing and spelling quite easy. Throughout my school days I always won at spelling.

Bitterne Church of England School

My schooling started as a five year old infant at a Church of England school. I soon learned that one of the advantages of going to a church school was that we had an extra holiday on Ascension Day. Furthermore, religion was taught every week, according to the school curriculum.

I remember the headmaster, Mr Shapley, the deputy head, Mr Whetton, Miss Mist, the oldest teacher, and Miss Penny.

At the age of seven, I moved up to the junior school. My teachers were Miss Drew, art, Miss Hayes, English and Mr Matthews, maths, history, geography and sport and Mr Stathan. At one of the parents' evenings Mr Matthews said to my mother that I was 'going nowhere'. What he meant I did not know because I was in the school chess team.

Under Mr Statham, we prepared ourselves for the eleven plus examination to determine our future education. Was it to be at a secondary modern school or a grammar school? Alas, in my case and despite my efforts, I failed the eleven plus and was selected to further my education at Merry Oak Secondary Modern Boys' School. Thankfully, I had done well enough to be placed in the top A stream at Merry Oak (there were four streams A,B, C and D) which would enable me to sit the GCE examinations, new to secondary schools.

I learnt that before this, only grammar school pupils could sit the GCE examinations. But due to a change in the examination structure, certain secondary modern schools would, under a new pilot scheme, be enabled to teach the curriculum. Merry Oak was one of those schools.

Whilst my parents shared my feelings about not passing the eleven plus, they realised that I was going to be given an opportunity to achieve something for my future and prove that I was not 'going nowhere'.

It was during this period of my education that there were a number of ground-breaking events elsewhere, which continue to be relevant today. These are but a few of them.

In July 1955, Ruth Ellis was the last woman to be hanged in Britain; shortly after that the last men were to follow. In March 1956, Pakistan became an Islamic Republic. In October 1956, Israeli armed forces invaded Egypt. In October 1957, Russia launched the first space satellite called Sputnik 1. In 1958, the first hovercraft was launched. The modern age was revving up its technological tentacles and spreading them very quickly.

Merry Oak Secondary Modern Boys' School

In September 1959, aged eleven and smartly dressed in a new school uniform of dark blue blazer with green piping around the edges and a compulsory cap in the same colours, I entered the gates of the school for the first time with the daunting prospect that I would be there for the next five years.

The gates had two prefects on them, whose job was to ensure that first year pupils wore the school cap when passing through the gates. Failure to do so would result in being marched to the office of the deputy head, Mr Edwards, for some sort of dressing down (pardon the pun). A practice soon developed with pupils who had no cap asking another pupil who had entered the school with their cap on to lob it over the hedge to enable the defaulter to enter the gates, cap on head, with no trouble at all!

Merry Oak had a reputation for being a tough boys' school. This led to a number of my friends from junior school being sent to other schools by their parents. In some contexts it was tough, as any boys' school might be, but I was never alarmed by this and, along with my parents, I had no problems, from start to finish. Boxing was still one of the sports activities in the school and I was quickly in the team.

The fact that some pupils could make things difficult, by bullying or fighting in the school precincts, was always promptly dealt with by the headmaster, Mr Ford. Although short in stature, he was big on discipline and soon earned the respect of those who crossed his path. On more than one occasion he executed his form of discipline by a public caning in front of the whole school.

I was selected for the highest stream, Tech. 1, the others being Tech. 2, 3 and 4. Furthermore, according to academic performance, a pupil could be promoted or demoted to another stream, normally at the end of the school year.

My first form teacher was Mr Charley (as he liked to be called) Sturgess. He taught English, maths and first level French (his wife was

French). I knew him from Bitterne School, where he taught my brother. He had film-star good looks and a jovial disposition, but if pushed too far would visit any troublesome pupil with a missile of chalk flying across the classroom in the right direction or, if more serious, delivering an old plimsoll forcefully to the backside, aiming the pupil's head towards the open door! Less serious transgressions resulted in one hundred lines of the longest non-technical English word, 'floccinaucinihilipilification'.

Overall, we respected him and his teaching was delivered with a theatrical, although genuinely serious, flourish, interspersed with vague references to Brigitte Bardot, his favourite film star of the day. That his style was theatrical is probably explained by his writing of the annual school pantomime and composing all of the songs. He was a consummate pianist and could play jazz and rag-time and give a great impression of Russ Conway, one of the most popular pianists of the time. Due to his style of teaching, I did well in both English and French. His end of year report about me said: 'A cheerful and willing boy who has worked well throughout the year. I am sure he will continue to maintain his high standard of work'.

During the first year I took part in the school sporting activities including athletics, football, cricket, shinty (a Gaelic form of hockey) and boxing and continued to do so throughout my school years, with the exception of boxing which was abolished. Furthermore, I was introduced to the rough and tumble playground game of Jeremiah one-two-three. Bums were sore!

This consisted of two teams of eight boys, one of which would form a line, each with their head between the legs of the boy in front until the first boy of the caterpillar of bent backs was locked between the legs of a boy standing with his back to the wall. The other team would then line up and, individually, run as fast as possible so as to land as far up the line of bent backs as possible. When the running team was all astride the bent team, they would them jump up and down on the line of bent backs chanting, 'Jeremiah, Jeremiah, one-two-three' until it collapsed. Punishing though it was, I continued playing this game until I left school.

My second year form teacher, Mr Stan Harding, was a bit of a surprise. He looked very young and could have passed for one of the boys. He taught English and got on with the whole class. In fact, his style of teaching was not only informed but very relaxed, making him very popular with everyone. My end of year report said: 'A quite well behaved boy, although he is inclined to be a little excitable. He seems to get on well with his classmates', and (for English) 'Has ability and should do well'.

The next two years at Merry Oak School were to be dominated by a different curriculum tailored to achieving success in the GCE examinations. This was a pilot scheme and we were to be the guinea pigs. Selection of subjects was based upon our strengths in them to date. My advanced subjects were English, English literature, maths, chemistry with physics, technical drawing and metalwork.

Thus, in my third year I found myself in the class of Mr Frost, a science and maths teacher.

My English Master was Mr Haydn Jones. He flew Pathfinder Bombers during the Second World War, in which he was awarded the Distinguished Flying Cross (DFC). He was a very clever and interesting man who inspired me in understanding the strength and depth of the English language. I really enjoyed his lessons.

He was responsible for the school library and after a while appointed me as one of the three librarians. This entailed the monitoring, and use, of the library by other pupils and looking after the lending and return of books.

Through Haydn Jones I became interested in the works of the great poets, especially Gerard Manley Hopkins, E. E. Cummings and T.S. Eliot, to name but a few. This was helped along by radio broadcasts in the classroom, such as Dylan Thomas' *Under Milk Wood*, delivered by the actor Richard Burton and revered at the time as the most original work for broadcasting in class. Inspired by this, I was determined to do well in the subject of English and, more importantly, the GCE examination.

Ironically, there was a twist in all of this. After I left school, my mother confided to me that Haydn Jones was married to her cousin Pat and was therefore a distant relative by marriage. I wonder if he ever knew that?

During the third year I represented the school at the Southampton Drama Festival in which I recited William Blake' s poem, *Tyger, Tyger burning bright, in the forests of the night; what immortal hand or eye could frame thy fearful symmetry....* for which I received a First Class Certificate. I also represented the school in athletics, taking part in hurdling, sprinting and the 880 yards race in which I came second.

At the end of the school year I was summoned to the headmaster's office for what I thought was some misdemeanour, only to find a number of my classmates there. After a short speech, he gave all of us prefect badges. Having been promoted, I had access to the prefect's room which had a cupboard laden with confiscated material such as packets of Woodbine cigarettes, sweets and risqué magazines of ladies in varying stages of undress. Being a prefect had its own, very enjoyable, privileges.

As one of the school librarians, I was also delegated to assist with the printing of the school magazine. A good job, very useful for my future!

My end of year report in the advanced subjects gave me good grades in English, including spelling, but not for the others. It concluded: 'He has made some progress throughout the year but has still much ground to make up, particularly in mathematics'.

So it was with some trepidation that I entered my fourth and final (exam) year in the class of Mr Slater, a stern maths teacher, although he did give me a lot of encouragement in my struggles with the subject, especially logarithms and geometry. Eventually I started to make some progress in the advanced subjects, in particular, that I had made 'Steady progress in (my) group'. Towards the end of the school year in 1964 I sat my GCE examinations and waited for the results.

Part 6
My career in law and first wife, Gloria —
1960 – 70

Starting out

In the early sixties and at the age of sixteen I set about finding a career. I was helped by the school careers master, Mr Lewry, who sent me to the Youth Careers Service in Southampton, for assessment. Whilst my ambitions were elsewhere (I wanted to be a telegraph engineer) I was given the opportunity of starting work as either a clerk with Readymade Concrete or as a law clerk with a firm of solicitors. In those days a career in law was largely the preserve of those who had a grammar school education leading to a university place.

The making of a lawyer

In 1963, I read an article in a Sunday newspaper that 'The Institute of Legal Executives (ILEX) had just been formed in place of the Solicitors' Managing Clerks Association', enabling those who did not have a university degree, or the means of getting one, to study law at night school and qualify as a lawyer through ILEX. This could be done through a new method called "Learn as you Earn".

Furthermore, the fellowship qualification was the same level as a LLB in law at a university. Interestingly, I noted from my research that Charles Dickens was employed by a firm of solicitors and became a freelance reporter of law cases between1827 and 1833. It looked to me that many of the people in his books were characteristic of those he saw in the courts at that time.

As a working-class boy this appealed to me and I promptly took up the offer of an interview at the law office of Stephens, Locke and Abel (SLA) Solicitors, in London Road, Southampton. They were in a row of Edwardian offices across the road facing the Ordnance Survey offices. I went through the door and there seemed to be an air of learned authority and the distinctive smell of old books, reminiscent I suppose of the writer, Dickens. I was immediately captured by the warmth of this.

The interview was conducted by the firm's partners, Harold Abel, Henry Howe and John Griffin. After some deliberation, I was offered the post of a trainee law clerk. Mr Abel was particularly impressed by those parts of my school leaving report stating that my 'integrity was undoubted' and that I was 'completely reliable... with good potentialities and the character to build a sound career'. As I left the office, John Griffin handed me a book, *Williams book on English Law*, to read. I found it so interesting that I read and returned it within two weeks. During the interview Harold Abel told me that clients came first at all times. I kept that in my head throughout my career.

After leaving school on the 4 August 1964, I rode my bike into the civil litigation department of SLA on a salary of £4.00 per week. Having been put in the deep end from the start, I looked forward to a challenging career in law.

Shortly after that I received my GCE exam results and had failed in every one of my four subjects. My parents and headmaster were very disappointed but luckily my employers were determined to keep me and try to make me something other than a non-qualified lawyer. John Griffin discussed this with me and my mother, as a result of which he immediately placed me at night school to retake my GCEs. English was all I needed. That done with a year's successful evening work at college I enrolled as a student with the institute on 27th July 1965 and started my law studies immediately. This was done at Southampton Technical College, in the evening initially, and then one afternoon each week.

Before departing from my school education, I would like to mention two interesting facts.

Firstly, the headmaster asked us in our last class to deliver a leaving essay on a historical character or nationality. I chose the history of the North American Indians (now Native Americans) to expand my knowledge. During my research I came across a Cherokee warrior named Sequoya. He was not educated as we are and could neither speak nor write in English, but listened to the pioneers walking through his lands. Over a period of twelve years he created and managed to produce, in 1821, an alphabet of Cherokee characters. This was adopted by the Cherokee nation and, months later, many of them could read and write. Having acquired a printing press, in 1828, they produced their own newspaper. I have a copy of their first printed alphabet.

Later in my life I had the privilege of visiting the American States of Georgia and South Carolina, their homelands, and seeing an open air play entitled *Unto these Hills*, written, directed and acted by a Cherokee cast. This was based upon what became known as the *Trail of Tears* when six thousand people, one quarter of the Cherokee nation, were displaced to Oklahoma against their wishes.

Secondly, in the period leading up to Christmas 1963, we had the pleasure of learning ballroom dancing with girls of our age, from the nearby Sholing Girls' School, every Friday afternoon. This was done in the hope that we were going to be decent young men. I have always liked music, singing and dancing, throughout my life. If anything, I found it is good therapy no matter your age or metier.

The coming of the sixties

More than any other decade after the Second World War, the 1960s developed into a time of dynamic changes and freedoms, which would influence the future of the world for many years to come. This was especially amongst the young people in many continents as seen when the Beatles hit Japan, Australia and the USA. In the western countries, the contraceptive pill and tights gave women liberation and was one of the first steps to feminism in equality of the sexes. Even more, it was a time when pop music, fashion and new ideas became important for everybody whilst having fun in a plethora of new colours and sounds.

For many men, National Service was coming to an end and the lid was being lifted for hordes of young people being fanned by the passions of independence and new experiences. For an example, I knew a number of mods from the services who used their discharge money on Lambretta and Vespa scooters. This was a hungry generation on the rise of a new Eden.

Over the pond in America, John Kennedy was the youngest man and first Roman Catholic to become president of the USA. He and his wife, Jackie, brought glamour and fashion to the White House, which quickly acquired the sobriquet of 'Camelot', the mythical court of King Arthur. Heads were starting to turn throughout the world.

In the same year, a more permissive era dawned, when the trial of the Crown against Penguin Books involving the notorious and allegedly obscene tale of *Lady Chatterley's Lover*, failed at the Old Bailey. The defence (Penguin) successfully convinced the jury that the prosecution case as to 'whether any man would want his wife or servant to read it', was out of touch with the times.

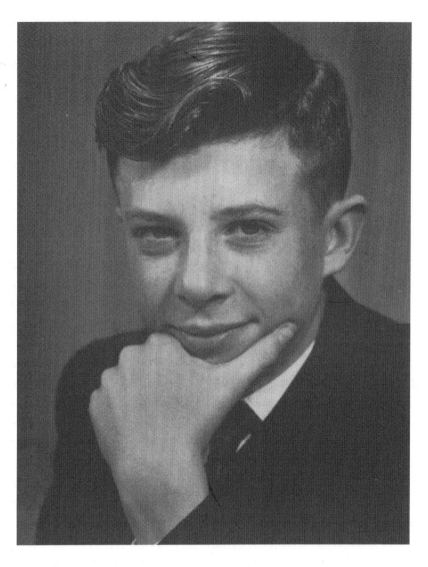

Peter with a quiff, aged thirteen

Somebody once said that, if you remembered what became known as the Swinging Sixties, you were never there. I can tell you now, that I was most certainly there and I remember exactly what it was like. It was a time never seen before as the curtains of the post-war years rolled open to reveal a colourful landscape of new light and vision, whether 'stoned' or not.

As my teens were approaching, I joined the Thornhill Youth Club. My attention was caught by the styles of clothes worn by Teddy boys and girls, jiving and dancing to the rhythm of rock and roll music. The Teddy boys' clothes consisted of tapered trousers and long colourful jackets. Their shoes were suede brothel-creepers or pointed winkle-pickers. Their style of dress was in contrast to the post-war look of sober clothes and suits. The girls were nicknamed 'Judies' and dressed in colourful T-shirts, circle skirts with stiff petticoats, white bobby-socks, dancing shoes and pony-tails. All of this had a big effect on me, and, at the age of twelve, I was the proud owner of a quiff and DA (duck's arse) hair style.

The subculture of rock and roll and other pop music, which started in the USA in the mid-1950s, was in full swing by 1960. The record charts were dominated by American singers such as Elvis Presley, Buddy Holly, Eddie Cochran, Jerry Lee Lewis and Little Richard, whose songs and styles were a mixture of raw, provocative Rock and Roll and mainstream pop in the form of ballads.

British popular music was dominated by skiffle stars such as Lonnie Donegan, Tommy Steele and Joe Brown, or mainstream pop stars like Cliff Richard and Marty Wilde amongst others. It was noticeable that some British stars emulated the American singers and their songs, like Buddy Holly and Johnny Cash. However, this was to change dramatically as the sixties unfolded.

Ironically, Gene Vincent was the first American rock and roll star to perform in Liverpool, wearing leathers, and a young man called John Lennon asked Billy Fury for his autograph after a show. Two wonderful examples of how the times were changing.

Throughout my life music has affected me. I never learnt to play a musical instrument well enough to make a career out of it. That, however, did not discourage me from taking a great interest in the different styles of music.

In 1960, under pressure from the rapidly changing times, the BBC launched the first pop music programme called *Saturday Club* hosted by the first DJ on Light radio, Brian Matthews. The programme was such an instant success, reaching out to a wider audience, that it quickly changed its name to *Easy Beat*, to match the type of music it was offering to an ever expanding audience, embracing not only the post-war generation but also a rapidly emerging and very hungry, younger but vibrant generation with new expectations, of which I was a very interested member.

My teens

On 4th January 1961, my thirteenth birthday, I became a teenager. Before 1900 the word teenager was unknown. The Victorians certainly never used it and young people between the ages of thirteen and nineteen were simply known as adolescents or juveniles. It was not until 1938 that the first mention of the word teenager was used to identify somebody from that age group. It became a badge of honour, worn with a rolling swagger, as famously demonstrated by the teen idol and late actor, James Dean. Having arrived at that seminal age, I knew I was on the first rung to adulthood.

During my teens I developed a mixture of views, interests and styles to suit the forever changing nature of my character and surroundings. For example, the self-styled teddy boy of my schooldays aged thirteen to sixteen (1961 to 1964), to the young beatnik part-time student aged sixteen to seventeen (1964 to 1965) and then as a modernist from 1965 onwards.

In April 1961, the Russian astronaut, Yuri Gagarin, made the first manned space flight. His successful return made him the first man to leave earth and thus trigger the race to space with the USA. At the same time, Russia helped Germany construct the Berlin Wall to be divided into the new states of West Germany, an ally of ours, and East Germany, a communist regime. On the home front, the new Archbishop of Canterbury, Dr. Ramsey, faced the problem of the nation's growing loss of interest in spiritual matters. Also in this year, Lady Diana Spencer was born (the future Princess of Wales) and at the end of the year, on the 10th December, Brian Epstein became the manager of the Beatles.

In the same year, my parents rented their first television with a fourteen inch black and white screen. We immediately started watching this and became familiar on a weekly basis with programmes like *The Avengers*, *Coronation Street*, *Thank Your Lucky Stars*, *Points Of View* and *Songs of Praise* along with *The Army Game* and *Emergency Ward*

Ten. From the USA we watched *The Lone Ranger*, *Seventy-Seven Sunset Strip* and *The Lucille Ball Show*, to name a few.

At the same time my mother's friend, Phyl, arrived from the USA for a holiday in England and, much to my mother's delight, visited us, together with her children Vicky, John, Lorna and Dana. Over the years, I got to know Phyl and her family through Christmas and birthday cards, some of which contained photographs of the children as they were growing up.

As a result of their visit, Vicky (a year younger than me) and I became pen-pals. This correspondence was to last over the next seventeen years. Following her graduation from high school, Vicky ended up as an intern in Washington and eventually returned to Pueblo, Colorado where she married the local sheriff. During that time, I became very fond of Vicky and our exchanges to each other were a wonderful building block in my life, reaching out to the world of our friendship.

Peter's American pen-pal, Vicky, in the 1960s

The Beatles rising

On New Year's Day 1962, The Beatles attended an audition, organised by their new manager, at the recording studio of the Decca Record Company, in London. Dick Rowe was the A & R manager at Decca, responsible for a new pop single production team, and attended the audition. The Beatles sang fifteen songs, three composed by Lennon/McCartney, commencing with *Like Dreamers Do*.

Sometime later in the following March, Dick Rowe called Brian Epstein and told him that Decca was not prepared to offer a contract to The Beatles. When asked for the reason, Dick Rowe said the (infamous words), "Sorry, Mr Epstein, but groups with guitars are on their way out." Three more recording companies, HMV, Pye and Columbia also turned them down. A short time later, Brian Epstein was introduced to George Martin, an A & R man at Parlophone Records, who was to eventually sign the band up to a recording contract with the Parlophone label. In August 1962, Ringo Starr replaced Pete Best as The Beatles drummer. The rest is history.

In 1962, my parents bought a red and white Dansette record player, complete with a stacking rod which could enable five records to be played automatically, one after the other. My brother and I thought that was really cool. At last we were able to hear our own music as chosen by each of us. Our parents bought a small number of 45 rpm records with the record player including our first pop record, *The Young Ones* by Cliff Richard. It was a warm summer's day. Immediately, Paul and I took out serious doses of saved pocket money and went up to the record shop in Bitterne. Towards the end of the year, we had a catalogue of records which we could each play and enjoy.

However, developments were taking place elsewhere in the world, which were to cast a shadow over our lives and which had been a constant threat to peace during the years of the Cold War between the USA and Russia. This was, of course, the Cuban missile crisis in October 1962 which took the human race to the brink of nuclear annihilation. It resulted in a tense stand-off between President John Kennedy of the USA and Nikita Khrushchev, the president of Russia. Neither could afford to lose face. Such a battle of wills was played out daily through the media of television news bulletins and in so doing, created in an atmosphere of real terror in our homes.

It was so serious that the headmaster of my school, Mr Ford, convened an assembly of the whole school to explain to us the nature and seriousness of the situation, so as to enable us to understand how this all came about and what was being done throughout the world to try and find a resolution. In the event, Russia capitulated by giving in to American demands to remove its missiles from Cuba, in return for America removing their missiles from Turkey. As young boys having lived through these historical events, our feelings veered from fear to relief and excitement that nuclear war had been averted and that the Americans, our allies, had exerted their power over communism. This was, arguably, the first step in bringing the Cold War to an end many years later.

During the same year the world was to lose one of the most famous and successful Hollywood film stars of all time. Born to a mother with mental illness and having a fractured childhood, Marilyn Monroe was to light up the world in numerous films from *The Asphalt Jungle* and *All about Eve* to *The Misfits* and *Some Like It Hot.* Sadly, such a legend was to die, aged thirty-six, from an alleged overdose of sleeping pills. The cause of Marilyn Monroe's death remains, to this day, a topic for discussion and conjecture, thereby enabling her to remain an everlasting icon in the history of the world. Towards the end of the year Nelson Mandela was jailed for inciting a national strike in South Africa.

At the same time The Beatles first record *Love me do* was played on the radio by Radio Luxembourg. It had an up and down run on the hit parade and on the 17th January 1963, the second record, *Please Please Me* took both records into the top of the charts. The rest is history.

Last but not least, satire became de rigueur as evidenced by the BBC television programme *That Was The Week That Was* of which I was to become an avid fan.

And so it was, that when I reached my fifteenth birthday in 1963, I felt that the world at large was a safer place and that somehow the future was going to change in a way that would sever our ties with the past in the most unexpected and exciting way. I refer of course, to what was to become…

The swinging sixties

Having regard to the many changes which were to define the future throughout the 1960s, there is still some debate as to when the 'Swinging Sixties' actually started. There is no doubt that it was either 1963 or 1964 and in my view, as somebody who was to play a part in it, there are a number of elements to support the argument either way.

For example, in the music world there was in 1963 an explosion of unique sounds never before heard in popular music. The sounds were raw, vibrant and imaginative emanating from the northern clubs, expanding rapidly throughout the country with such intensity, that before long London was firmly positioned as the capital of popular music worldwide.

The upsurge of numerous pop bands consisting of a new generation of creative youngsters belting out tunes through the excesses and versatility of the new style of electric guitars, such as the Rickenbacker, complemented by a tympanum of tightly drawn drums and Hammond organs, overwhelming the hitherto dominance of American popular music.

The outcome and popularity of this upsurge of national talent was such that by the end of 1963 British performers were able to amass eighteen number one hits in the popular music charts, led strongly by The Beatles, against one such hit from America, performed inevitably by Elvis Presley. Not only did this abundance of superiority enormously increase the production and sale of electric guitars and other correlated instruments, but it also resulted in numerous clubs and other venues, such as Top Rank and Mecca, springing up throughout Britain to absorb this new phenomenon and its young following called 'youth' (more of this later).

In August 1963, the television station ITV transmitted for the first time a popular music show, *Ready Steady Go!* It was youth-orientated and shown weekly on Friday evenings until December 1966. The presenters were Keith Fordyce and Cathy McGowan, a mod girl wearing the latest in designer clothes of the time. She reflected the youthful enthusiasm for the popular performers of the the time, such as The Who, Manfred Mann, The Hollies and Dusty Springfield. Initially, some of the performing artists mimed their lyrics, a practice which continued until the end of 1964. I was an avid fan of the show, which was unique in its good vibration, illustrating beyond doubt that *The Times They Are a-Changing*, an anthem of the time by the American troubadour, Bob Dylan, now a legend.

As part of these events a somewhat brash and hopeful group of five teen school boys formed a band called The Pacifics. The line-up of the band was Geoff Butt, Ian Taylor, Alan Wells, Allan Withers and me, as the singer. We thought we could be a big noise in popular music! We had the permission of the headmaster to practice and rehearse our performances in the school premises, usually at lunch times in the assembly hall and, on a Saturday morning, begrudgingly so far as the caretaker was concerned, in the school music room. The headmaster was, I think, a bit bemused by our renditions of popular songs of the day (such as The Beatles), as he passed through the hall with a wry smile. Inevitably, our sound drew an audience of schoolboys from the playground peering in through the windows. What they made of our efforts I do not know, but we did get some claps from them. The trouble was, that we wanted to be a 'big noise' pounding out our versions of The Beatles songs and other rock and roll numbers, but we needed plenty of practice. We also lacked the latest instruments and realised we needed to pool some money to obtain these. As we progressed we needed to have more room to practice in and did so at each other's homes, usually in the evening.

The assassination of President John Kennedy

It was during one of these practice sessions on a cold autumn evening at Allan Withers' house that we were told by his mother that the American President John Kennedy had been shot. The date was 23rd November 1963 and Mrs Withers was in shock, with tears in her eyes. We stopped playing immediately so that we could take in what we had just been told. It seemed that the world had come to a stop and taken in a deep breath of disbelief.

At home I joined my family in watching the TV news bulletins broadcasted live from America, as the drama unfolded into the night. After what seemed an eternity, the TV commentator confirmed that Kennedy was dead. We were totally numbed. Bearing in mind the young John Kennedy had just saved the world in the Cuban crisis against Russia, we tried to gather our thoughts realising that all the hope which the young president had brought to the world was going to be crushed. In such circumstances it is a truism that you knew exactly where you were and what you were doing at that time; I was practising with The Pacifics! The world trembled!

In the field of politics, another news item in 1963 stirred the interest of the public and that was the Profumo affair. This involved the Minister for War of the Tory Government, John Profumo, who was having an affair with Christine Keeler, a call girl. The other players in this intrigue were Dr Steven Ward, who introduced them to each other, Mandy Rice-Davies, an acquaintance of Keeler, and Eugene Ivanov, a Russian naval attache, with whom Christine was also having an affair. Whilst being tried for allegedly living off immoral earnings, Dr Steven Ward, an important witness, committed suicide, feeling that he had been let down by the justice system. Immediately, an inquiry of these events was entrusted to Lord Denning, the Master of the Rolls.

These two events posed security risks to our nation. The Tories were in disarray, whilst in one of his last speeches, President Kennedy stated "this is a dangerous and uncertain world". This whole scenario was played out at the highest levels of society and brought into question the morals of that social order as well as the integrity of the government which, within a year, was to be swept from power after ruling for thirteen years, to be replaced by the Labour Party.

To ice the cake, in the same year the great train robbery took place, when an unknown number of men stole £2,631,784.00 from the London to Glasgow mail train, the largest sum of money ever stolen at the time.

By 1964 it was evident that society was rapidly moving away from the old order of post-war Britain and that events were making way for a new class of young people with refreshing ideas, driven and defined by the media as "The Youth Culture". The words 'Fab' and 'groovy' became part of the language of fashionable people. There was a reason to loosen up. The cinemas were showing films like *The Italian Job* and *Alfie*. The actor in both was Michael Caine, who would go on to make many great films.

Musically, it was clear that the front runners in the development of this culture were The Beatles and their only real rivals, The Rolling Stones. Evidence of this was in 1963 when the Beatles had three enormous pop hits, *Please Please Me*, *I Want To Hold Your Hand* and *She Loves You* (which alone had advance orders of half a million, a record in the history of popular music). As a result of this and the gigantic popularity of the band, Beatlemania became a phenomenon throughout the world and would last from 1964 until 1966.

Later in the year, when The Beatles appeared at the Royal Command Variety Performance in London, there was a television audience of twenty-eight million and in America, when the band appeared on the Ed Sullivan Show, the television audience was seventy-three million. Furthermore, The Beatles had five top positions in the US Billboard singles chart. By then, The Beatles image was that of four young lads from Liverpool, with mop-hair, smart suits, white shirts with ties complemented by winklepicker boots with Cuban heels. In contrast, The Rolling Stones were more anarchic and anti-establishment, wearing the diverse and more relaxed attire of art students.

In January 1964 the BBC launched its own popular television show *Top Of The Pops*, which was transmitted on Thursday nights. It was inspired by the *Teen and Twenty Club* on Radio Luxembourg and was presented initially by Jimmy Savile and Alan Freeman. It was also youth-orientated, as was RSG, but with more studio audience participation. Again, it attracted the popular artists of those times and was to continue doing so until 2006, in the case of *Top Of The Pops*. Throughout those times we have listened to a horde of great DJs from Kenny Everett, at Radio London to Tony Blackburn on Radio Caroline, both pirate stations until they were banned in 1968.

All of these brought to us the freeloading Brit pop of the sixties, glam rock of the seventies, punk rock of the late seventies/early eighties, romantic rock of the nineties, right up to the derivative retro rock of today. I still love music (popular and classical), singing and dancing.

All of these factors made an important contribution towards the real phenomenon known as the swinging sixties. This was quickly joined by the new darlings of fashion.

In 1964, Mary Quant designed the mini-skirt, which was to set the style and change fashion for young women in the western world forever. It defined a generation of young people known as mods, who would sit comfortably alongside other popular designers of the decade.

These included the French designer Andre Courreges, who introduced, amongst other styles, box-shaped dresses in fluorescent colours, white PVC boots and fashion goggles. In May 1964, Barbara Hulanicki, who founded the Biba fashion house with her husband, Stephen Fitz-Simon, had her first success selling dresses through her postal boutique. The boutique was so successful, that in September 1964 the first Biba store was opened in Kensington, London. The Biba style, involving earthy colours, was sold against the art-deco interior of the store and became a resounding success, which still survives to this day.

Furthermore, in the mid-1960s onwards, Carnaby Street and the Kings Road, London were like magnetic catwalks where people of all shapes, sizes and tastes would walk up and down the street, parading their latest styles both in fashion and looks. Women would be inspired by the popular models of the day such as Jean Shrimpton, Twiggy, Penelope Tree and Veruschka, amongst others. It was in that time bell-bottom" trousers became very popular and would eventually be worn by men and women. I visited London on many occasions in the sixties enjoying the atmosphere and became a mod. My brother Paul followed me and we would share our mod clothes when we were going out to hit the town. We were real kingpins!

In addition, new styles for the modern home and interiors were developed by Terence Conran and his household store Habitat soon became very popular with the new generation.

Having reached the age of sixteen I went out with my first girlfriend. Her name was Jane. She was a pretty blonde and fifteen years old. After a few dates strolling along Weston Shore watching the movements of shipping and other watercrafts going up and down the Solent, I was introduced to her parents who had a grocery shop with their flat above it. On some evenings Jane and I would stay in and listen to John Peel on his Luxembourg pop station or go to the local cinema. On one of those occasions her parents took us for dinner at a local Chinese restaurant. This was the first time I had Chinese food. Unfortunately, jitters in my stomach started. Having had only my mother's traditional English food, I struggled with the menu. Egg foo yung and chow mein meant nothing to me. I was a real Chinese food virgin and ended up with a chicken egg foo yung. Later I got to enjoy the food because the girl I was dating liked it.

At the same time the Pacifics had folded (Allan Withers having emigrated with his family to Australia). I lost interest in becoming a rock star and concentrated on my burgeoning career in law. This seemed to be more interesting to talk about with my girlfriends. One topic stood out in the newspapers that time.

In August 1964, two murderers named Peter Allen and Gwynne Evans were the last to be executed in the United Kingdom. However, it was not until 1969 that the death penalty was finally abolished and capital punishment was taken off the law books of England and Wales.

With money in my pocket from a newspaper round I was doing in the last year at school, I was able to build up my first collection of pop records. My musical tastes at that time were assisted by tuning into AFN (the American Forces Network), from which I began to take more interest in American roots music such as the blues. This resulted in me spending my hard earned money on music albums, not only by The Beatles, but also by American artists such as Hank Williams, Slim Whitman, Johnny

Cash, Paul Simon, Dave Brubeck, Joan Baez and Jesse Fuller. Canada had their troubadour, Leonard Cohen. I ended up being a great fan of The Boss, Bruce Springsteen, whose lyrics and music seem to hit the hearts of the working class. On my sixtieth birthday Lizzie and I went to see him playing at the football ground of Arsenal FC, paid for by my daughters Emma and Anna; he almost blew the roof off, right from the start. What a man!

I was also interested in the ever-increasing soul music emanating from America, through the labels Motown and Stax and great singers including Sam Cook, Otis Redding, Marvin Gay, Aretha Franklin, Martha and the Vandellas, Gladys Knight and the Pips, The Marvellettes, Four Tops and Temptations. In addition, Carole King is one of the greatest songwriters and singers in the musical world as shown by her legendary album, Tapestry.

In June 1964, Nelson Mandela was sentenced to life in South Africa on a charge of treason and in the following month, President Johnson signed the Civil Rights Act, abolishing segregation in the USA.

Towards the end of the year, I went to see The Soul Agents (a local band) playing live at Tauntons Grammar School in Southampton. The Agents' music was pure soul and they could boast being the warm up band when on tour with the likes of the Rolling Stones and Booker T and the MGs, amongst others. The Agents' line-up included Johnny Keeping, Jim Bach, Don Shinn and Roger Pope (all of whom would be successful in varying degrees). At one stage the band included a singer named Rod 'the Mod' Stewart with whom, some years later, I had the opportunity to have a chat. He, of course, went on to greater fame. On the same note, I got to know Johnny Keeping's father as a client of the law firm with whom I was training. It is also sad to reflect that Roger Pope died in September 2013, having achieved fame as the drummer with Elton John.

In December 1964, Sam Cook was to suffer a violent death in very suspicious circumstances which still remain unanswered. One of my favourite soul singers, his unique style was to influence numerous singers and bands in the years to come, thereby ensuring his legendary status as the pioneer of soul.

In the same month, Martin Luther King, who was responsible for pioneering the Civil Rights Movement in the USA, was awarded the

Nobel Prize for Peace; whilst America was still embroiled in dealing with ongoing unrest in its southern states and a disastrous war in Vietnam. All of this whilst a new Britain was emerging.

The death of Winston Churchill

The 25th January 1965 started with the death of Winston Churchill who in my opinion, was one of the finest prime ministers in history. In February I watched his state funeral on television. Never before had I seen such a moving spectacle befitting a man of the people, who saved our nation at a time of great fear and deprivation from a brutal enemy.

It was the mid-point of the decade and at the age of seventeen I found the Mighty Acorn, a cafe bar across the road from the college at which I gained my GCE qualification and started my legal studies. The cafe bar catered for a crowd of charismatic bohemians and students who created a lively atmosphere, helped along by the addictive aroma of strong coffee and weed. I suspect that my passive introduction to drugs had some effect upon my demeanour in embracing my new found environment. The bar music was jazz, soul and blues with occasional live singers and musicians. Captivated by this culture, I changed my own recreational style by dressing in casual fine cord trousers, sloppy jumpers, maroon suede calf length boots and a donkey jacket which my father obtained from the docks! Added to this I let my hair grow and, after a while, found myself fully enjoying this new found freedom of expression.

At the same time my interest in poetry started to go into overdrive, resulting in the purchase, over the next few years, of a number of books published by Penguin Modern Poets including Ferlinghetti, Ginsberg, Henri, McGough, Patten and Enzesberger and separate books by Yevteshenko, Holub, Akhmatova, Libby Houston, EE Cummings, Jacques Prevert and Dylan Thomas. These were complemented by *The Faber Book of Modern Verse* and the *Methuen Anthology of Modern Verse 1940–1960*. I regularly frequented the October Bookshop in the St. Mary's district of Southampton as my source of all types of literature, controversial or otherwise. This rich seam of international authors quickly broadened my knowledge and included books written by Che Guevera, Marx and Lenin as well as Freud and Nietzsche. As to novels, my tastes at the time leaned largely to the Russian writers, such as Dostoyevsky and Pushkin.

Having come from a working class background and armed with all this material, I started to attend the Young Socialists meetings simply because my philosophy was that any person who had to work to survive was working class, although I found the class system very unsettling as we are all born equal. In time this brought me into conflict with some of the extreme political philosophies of the Young Socialists, such as 'the state will provide' and so I left to move on to new pastures.

With so many ideas now giving me direction in my life and in part as a result of the growing youth culture, I joined Moorhill Youth Club based at Moorhill School. From that I was quickly co-opted on to the club committee. Following that appointment, I soon became editor of the Youth Magazine and was then voted on to the Southampton Borough City Youth Council. This met four times a year at the borough council's chamber in the civic centre and provided a voice for the youth of Southampton, having regard to the challenges then facing youngsters, such as the rising drug culture and free permissive behaviour. To further make myself known around Southampton, I became a member of the Wayfarers Dramatic Society.

In the spring of 1965, I had a new girlfriend. Her name was Marilyn and she was a pupil at Itchen Grammar School. She was very attractive and had a voluptuous figure. I first noticed her when I was making my way home after a day's work. She and her friend, Christine, were sitting on the next door neighbour's brick wall. Upon seeing me, they would both burst into a fit of giggles. This became a frequent occurrence until one day Christine approached me and said that Marilyn wanted to know if I had a girlfriend. I told Christine that if Marilyn wanted to know she should ask me. This she did and we started to go out with each other in a light fashion. Marilyn was very bright, knowledgeable and good company. She was enthusiastic about my legal career as well as many other things which interested her. After a while I started calling at her home, which was a short walk away on the same estate, and we would go for long walks or to the bowling alley in Bitterne village.

One Saturday afternoon I called for Marilyn and upon greeting me she surprised me with my first French kiss. She wanted more from the relationship and I had no difficulty with that as I was growing very fond of her. However, on this particular occasion, when Marilyn was out of the room, her father approached me and asked how old I was. Upon telling him that I was seventeen, he told me that Marilyn was only thirteen years of age. I was taken aback by this because she was looked at least fifteen to me! However, much as I was very fond of Marilyn, I told her that I did not think the relationship could go very much further, other than as friends. I continued to see Marilyn at the bowling alley, but with less frequency and eventually our close friendship came to an end. Some years later, I saw Marilyn shopping in the town centre. She had become a very beautiful woman, had a good career and was married, but told me that I was her very first true love, never forgotten. She kissed me on the cheek and walked away smiling.

One of the Moorhill Club committee members was Colin Sampson, an art teacher and school representative. He drove a 1930s three-wheeled, two-seater, Morgan open-top sports car and wore a Second World War leather flying hat and goggles. He was a very interesting character and was married to Sylvie, another art teacher. I got to know them so well that Colin would occasionally give me a lift home from the club. I can honestly say that travelling in a vintage three-wheeled sports car in the cool of the summer night was an experience I have forever cherished. It gave me a feeling of freedom and adventure, even more so when I was squashed in the back boot when Sylvie was in the front passenger seat. As I got to know them more, Colin and Sylvie would invite me to supper at their flat in Woolston.

They were a truly bohemian couple who mixed with a similar crowd and with which with I started to mingle. These visits to their home resulted in me savouring Sylvie's Spanish omelettes, a novelty to me, and meeting Michael Lawrence, a fellow English teacher and poet. I still have his book of poems, *A Stone In The Eye of the Sun* which would later inspire me to take up writing poetry.

On one of my outings with Colin, Sylvie and Michael, we went with some of their other friends to the Classic Cinema in Southampton, where the film *Ulysses*, from the book by James Joyce was having a private viewing. It was an extremely controversial film touching upon temptation and inappropriate behaviour within the Catholic faith in Ireland and was banned from mainstream circulation.

Whilst my friendship with Colin and Sylvie was to continue into the late sixties (they eventually separated), my ambitions were steering me in other directions.

Following my attendance at Southampton University for a live performance of John Mayall's Bluesbreakers, my interest in music and singing was increased. The line-up of the band at the time included John McVie, Mick Fleetwood and Eric Clapton and I was blown away by their performances. Mcvie and Fleetood would become part of the ground-breaking band, Fleetwood Mac, whist Clapton would appear again with bands such as the Yardbirds and Cream, before carving out his own sensational career. Incidentally, I got into the concert by persuading a hapless student at the door to give me a ticket without any hesitation, by letting him think that I was with the band! At that time I was still a bohemian and must have looked the part. It was at the university I saw Pete Seger and Julie Felix giving the audience a chance of singing with them on the stage. It was a warm summer night and everybody joined in with his seminal song, *Where have all the flowers gone*. It is one of my favourite songs.

In my desire to look the part as a mod, I purchased a 1957 Lambretta motor scooter from a colleague at work. It had a faulty first gear, but that compared to the bright blue colour and painted American eagles on each pannier together with a shotgun (noisy) exhaust and three other gears, was of no consequence. With the right clothes, I was soon transformed into one of the scooter-riding versions of a real Mod, the only exception being that I never wanted a parka. I did, however, wear a Madras jacket with Ben Sherman T-shirt, Levi jeans and an American soldier's peaked cap with an eagle clasp holding up the peak. With that ensemble on one summer's evening, I was sitting on my scooter when a lad on his moped challenged me to a race. Immediately, we revved off at great speed together. With a big noise and at full throttle the Lambretta won. Fab!

Now that I was independently mobile the world became my oyster. I could quickly move from one mod venue to another which had the result of increasing my social circle. For some reason, the newly built bowling alley in Bitterne was a magnet for the mod culture with numerous mod scooters in all their chromatic glory lined up alongside the edge of the road. Before long I was running around town with a passenger, male or female, going to various events.

The bowling alley had its own Pinball Machine and in no time, I became the pinball wizard! When I started to play, a crowd would gather round and the jukebox would be playing *Ain't too proud to beg* by the Temptations, in the background. The atmosphere was electric, with stimulants all around.

It was through these channels that I heard about the Concorde Club in Burgess Road. It was a jazz club owned by a musician named Cole Mathieson, but word got around that performers such as Manfred Mann and The Bryan Auger Trinity, favoured by the mods, were regular features. I therefore joined the club, not knowing the membership was eighteen plus!

Later in the year, two female staff members of the staff in the office where I worked, visited me in lunch time and started talking to me about sex; I did not know how to respond. I actually found it amusing. Afterwards one of the head secretaries said they were testing how much of an innocent abroad I was. They were both very attractive and shortly after, I took one of them on a date. This is a simple example of behaviour at work, which was regarded as fun in the 1960s, but would not be tolerated in today's society of political correctness.

On the run

As well as my first mentor in the law, John Griffin was a Scoutmaster to a troop of Sea Scouts. He prided himself in having a number of sit-up-and-beg bicycles with grocery baskets for his troop and he rode one into work each day. What the Scouts did with all the other bikes I am not quite sure, but he was always using them. As Sea Scouts I know they often went white-water rafting in places such as Canada. I would have liked to join them but my law studies came first.

One day John asked me to help him to set up a search and recognise exercise for his troop of scouts. He wanted me to participate by being the target for what the scouts had to do. John had a great imagination and wanted to superimpose a photo-image of me as a criminal on criminal records office notepaper. The idea was that one evening I would board a train at Bitterne railway station bound for Portsmouth. I would then randomly visit a number of cafes in Southsea and the scouts were to try and seek me out and log where I was found. On the photograph John gave to me I was prisoner number 942622 on the run and I had to stop shaving for a while so as to grow a morning shadow to make my profile on the photograph a bit more realistic looking like a convict on the run.

Come the day, I made the rail journey to Southsea and placed myself in the designated cafés. I was not to know when the scouts had spotted me. As the evening moved on, I was conscious of the fact that I needed to get back home and not to miss the last train. I need not worry.

Towards the end of the evening I was approached in the cafe by two 'police officers' in uniform who asked if I was Peter Chainey, as shown on the CRO notepaper they were holding. I said I was and they said I was 'nicked'. This was in front of a cafe full of people. I was quickly ushered out to a waiting police car and taken to a local police station. There I was placed in a cell. After a while and with a big smile on his face, John Griffin arrived and one of the police officers introduced him as my lawyer. Settling down into a comfortable journey back to Southampton in John's car, we both had a good laugh and discussion about how well it went, including my faked arrest and CRO number! At the end, drinks and sandwiches rounded off the evening and to me the theme and method was good character-building for law.

Peter having fun in his first job in the law

The end of the working year was celebrated in the most unlikely of venues. Throughout the year I had attended Southampton County Court virtually every day of the week, either to issue proceedings or enforce the processes of litigation, such as writs, summonses, petitions and warrants to attend court hearings either with counsel, or personally, on behalf of my clients. In so doing, I got to know a number of the court staff very well, in particular the female staff, one of whom was a very famous beauty queen. Christmas was looming and members of the legal profession were invited to join the staff and judges at the court's annual Christmas party at the end of the day.

Upon arrival with some of my colleagues from our firm I was amazed to see the court offices adorned with decorations and mistletoe, with food and drinks being served from desks and public service counters. The party was in full swing with music blaring out and the female staff were dressed in their finery. As the evening progressed and with drinks flowing freely, the atmosphere soon changed. At that point the judges left.

Caution was then thrown to the wind, to be replaced by an air of abandon and anything goes! Snogging anybody and people running up and down the corridors and stairs in the court complex. Some did not return for some time! It was out of this maelstrom that my next girlfriend emerged. Her name was Jenny and she was a right-on mod. She was a court clerk in the family section, but more of this later. Needless to say, I made my way home from the court that night not knowing what time of the day it was or what I got up to!

Those were the days!

Contrary to the stuffy perception of the legal profession, I realised that my journey in the practice of law promised to be eventful, challenging and full of surprises, which it turned out to be.

In 1965 I asked one of the partners why there were no female partners in the office and it seemed in others. His brief response was that they might take maternity leave in the future. Historically, the first female solicitor in practice was Mary Sykes in 1922. Going forward in 2012 there were more female solicitors than men in practice, many of whom were partners!

In early 1966 I had to take some papers to another solicitor, Cecil Paris of Paris Smith and Randall. After we concluded our business, I remarked about the cricket trophies in his office. He asked if I liked cricket, which I did, and we were then engaged in a very interesting discussion on the sport. I was thrilled when Cecil Paris told me that during the second World War he was a liaison officer with the 21st Group for General Bernard Montgomery. Later, I found out that Cecil Paris was awarded the Czechoslovack War Cross. He played for Hampshire

Cricket Club between 1933–1948 and died on 4th April 1998. I found him to be a very interesting lawyer and helpful in the business we were dealing with.

In the same year I went to see my first case in the high court at the Great Hall, Winchester with John Griffin and a barrister. I was carrying the barrister's bag containing his robe, collar and wig; he was carrying his case papers in his travelling bag. I was eighteen years old and it was an importuning offence involving one male offender who unfortunately was the chauffer of an African president. We were acting for the ambassador of the country and declaring diplomatic immunity! I found it very interesting, my first day, on the nature of the case, on the sanctity of the court room and people dealing with the case, that is the judge, the lawyers, the ambassador, the accused and witnesses; all being looked upon by the majesty of Queen Victoria's statue and the round table of King Arthur! I was in awe and inspired.

In the same year I was taking judgment summons to the Southampton County Court for bad debts. If there was a default the debtor would go to prison for six weeks immediately. If the debtors needed help 1 would direct them to the Legal Aid office in Brunswick Road just around the corner from my office or get help from a lawyer. The abolition of going to prison for debt was made long ago.

After of the first year of my job and having learnt it quickly, John Griffin started training me to be a legal costs draftsman to run alongside the outcomes of cases. Solicitors were not trained to do this in their curriculums but legal executives would be able to do so elsewhere. John Griffin also started me reading the monthly magazine, *Forensics and the Law*. He said this would help me for injury/accident cases in the future.

A touch of Dickens

Still in my teens, there were three other legal executives in the firm, all of whom did non-contentious work. Their names were George Macklin, Ron Merrick and Dennis Forrest. George and Ron were advanced in years and told me many stories about their times in the law in the late Victorian and Edwardian days. I was in awe of them and they taught me how to make quill feather pens. Their desks had many of those pens on them, together with ink pots and sealing wax. I really felt I was in the land of Dickens. Before long I could shave the tip of the pen to suit the dimension of the nib for the particular job in hand. I used it mainly for chancery or probate cases and used sealing wax for papers as necessary. Obviously this was all before the advent of word processing and technology.

Elsewhere in 1965, the Beatles were awarded MBEs individually, the first and only pop band to achieve this in such a short time. This caused much blustering from previous recipients who would return their medals feeling that the award had been devalued. It was, however, the first gesture from the highest level of society whereby the establishment recognised the new order driven by the culture of youth. Much later, in November 1969, John Lennon would return his medal to the queen stating, amongst other things, that he had sold out to the establishment. By then he was heavily influenced by Yoko Ono, his wife, during the period of their peace protests.

As for me, the year opened up numerous opportunities and much hope of achievement in my chosen career and way of life. I was deep in my studies, not only with the law papers from the institute and college, but at Southampton University law library, also. It was at this time that I decided to go into contentious litigation as opposed to non-contentious. I felt that this would be more challenging and exciting.

To balance out my studies, I broadened my interest in girls, which in turn led to me developing a great interest in watching films whilst courting them. During the year, accompanied by the latest girlfriend, I remember seeing the *Sound of Music* (five times with five different girls), *Dr Zhivago, Thunderball, For a Few Dollars More, Those Magnificent Men in their Flying Machines, The Spy Who Came in From The Cold, The Greatest Story Ever Told, What's New Pussycat* and *Darling* plus many others. At this time in my life, I seldom dated a girl for more than a week.

In 1966, the England football team won the World Cup against Germany. This brought another well-deserved dimension and glow of pride to the swinging sixties, which has not since been repeated.

It was also the year when, virtually every weekend on a Saturday, Paul and I, together with our regular group of mods, hit the terraces at the Dell football ground to watch our team, Southampton, play a home game. Our chosen position on the terraces was at the Milton Road end, where a lively afternoon's entertainment would be guaranteed, mainly because the opposing team's fans would also congregate there. Passions ran high, leading to aggressive behaviour and punch-ups amongst the spectators. In addition to the football, my brother and I found this very entertaining, but very seldom got involved in the fracas. At the end of a Saturday afternoon we were tanked-up to hit the bars in readiness for an evening at the Top Rank or the Mecca Ballroom on Southampton Pier.

During the same year I made good use of my membership at the Concorde Club by attending the club every week on a Tuesday and/or Thursday. It was usually packed, with mods, and a guaranteed sell-out when bands like Simon Dupree and the Big Sound, The Steam Packet comprising The Brian Augur Trinity, Julie Driscoll, Long John Baldry and Rod Stewart and The Grease Band including Joe Cocker were performing. They were all regulars and on one occasion I got to rub shoulders again with Rod the Mod at the bar when we were each ordering drinks. I also went on blues nights where I got to meet and spend a bit of time speaking with the American blues singer, Jesse Fuller, who produced the most amazing sounds from his one-man band, steel guitar and harmonica. It was called San Francisco blues and after his set, I spoke with him for a while and got his autograph. I also bought one of his albums.

Social life at the club resulted in many friendships being made, both male and female, and in no time, I was part of a regular group of mods comprising Stewart Clark, Geoff Mullins, Les Hamilton and Dave Wareham. We not only frequented the Dell, Concorde Club, Mecca and Top Rank ballrooms but also the coffee bars at the Bargate and Kasbah in the centre of Southampton. When my brother, Paul, joined us we also met up at the U25 Club at the Ordnance Survey, where he was working. Clubs were springing up everywhere over the country.

Gradually, I got to know Jenny from my frequent visits to the county court and as we approached the spring we became an item. She was seventeen years old with a strong northern accent and a quirky sense of humour. She was open-minded and embraced the freedom of the contraceptive pill. Wearing the shortest of miniskirts, she would ride pillion on my scooter regardless of the fact that, in common with other mod girls, the exposure of her legs left little to the imagination. Jenny, who lived with her mother in Bitterne Manor, was great fun, enjoyed clubbing, going to parties and nights in listening to music. As a girl from the Wirral, she was an avid fan of The Beatles and other bands from Liverpool. We had a shared interest in the rock music of some of the more prominent and creative American bands, particularly The Byrds and Loving Spoonful. This was engendered by the release in May 1966 of the Beach Boys greatest album *Pet Sounds*, incorporating such classic numbers as *God Only Knows*, *Wouldn't It Be Nice* and, one of my favourites, *Sloop John B*. The *Sounds* reflected the emergence of psychedelic rock sounds and Californian lifestyle as a whole.

As our time together moved on, it was clear that Jenny wanted commitment, but at just eighteen years of age I was not ready for this. After three months I started to cool the relationship even though I still had some feelings for her. It was at this point that fate played its hand. Without warning, Jenny became very ill and was rushed to hospital. She was diagnosed with peritonitis, a life-threatening condition, and had to undergo a number of gruelling operations over a lengthy period of time. Because of my feelings for Jenny, I could not bring myself to abandon her and started visiting her in hospital on a regular basis. Jenny's recovery was very slow and as the weeks passed by it was clear that she was not going to be discharged from hospital for some time. Having resigned herself to the situation, we both agreed to part company so as to enable Jenny to focus all her efforts on making that recovery. I believe that a little later she and her mother returned to the Wirral.

Throughout this period, I continued going out with my brother and other friends, attending meetings at the youth club and council, plus my law studies at the college. In addition to those studies, John Griffin arranged for me to attend weekly sessions at the local law centres, assisting in and giving free legal advice to those who most needed, but could not afford it. The centre was in one of the run-down areas of Southampton and I found the whole experience humbling, but enlightening, as the attendees ranged from the very poor, those in need of help with benefits and others with serious drug problems. On top of that, I had regular visits from prostitutes, some of whom were only fourteen years old.

At this time I was training on Admiralty Court civil cases which I found very adventurous. Because Southampton had a marine port, I could chart the coming and going of shipping within its waters. My admiralty cases, for example collisions, damage to cargo, salvage, claimants' property such as yachts and any other illegal actions at sea would be dealt with in the admiralty division of the high court. The course of action could be 'arrested'. On a number of times I saw the admiralty marshal boat chasing a vessel trying to get in or out of our waters illegally under a court warrant. On a number of times I went with the marshal in his boat to affix the court warrant on the vessel under the eyes of him. I enjoyed seeing justice being done under and over our seas.

As I have said my sister, Catherine, was born on 4th September 1966. She was clearly the daughter my mother always wanted to have and was welcomed with great joy. Following Catherine's birth and during her formative years, she was treated by my parents like an only child. Of course, both Paul and I were in our late teens and seldom at home due to work commitments and our respective social lives. I was eighteen when Catherine was born. As she grew up she ploughed her own furrow until she married and had two children, Nicholas and Saskia. I keep in touch with Catherine and her family through the exchange of Christmas and birthday cards. She lives in Chandlers Ford as well.

Aberfan, a Welsh tragedy

In October 1966, we were all shocked by the news that one hundred and sixteen children were killed when a coal tip collapsed on a school in the mining village of Aberfan, Wales. The shock waves rolled on well into the New Year and evermore in the hearts of the Welsh. The minister of Wales said a generation of their children "had been wiped out". Some years later I visited Wales on holiday and in homage went to the village. I was stunned by the silence and the memorial to those lost brought tears to my eyes.

In January 1967, a TV film called *Cathy Come Home* caused a public outcry. It was the story of a homeless mother with an infant child. Her only refuge was an unsuitable women's hostel. The clear message of the story was one of human misery at the most vulnerable level and highlighted what was then a national scandal, brought to the attention of the viewing public for the first time. It was in such a forceful and realistic way that it was eventually responsible for creating the charity Shelter.

Although not entirely similar, I can recall two cases myself in which the lonely mother and child scenario could have ended in great heartache, but didn't.

The first involved a close neighbour's teenage daughter being sent away from home to a convent because she was expecting a baby. The result of what was then considered a scandal and therefore hushed up, would ordinarily have been be to put the child out for adoption, never to be seen again by the mother. However, in this particular case, the mother refused to give up her child (a daughter) and both returned back home some time later, with the full support and understanding of her family.

The second concerned a cousin, who found herself in a similar position and, notwithstanding the perception of others and the mores of the times, was fully embraced, with her child, by her parents, who were willing without question to assist in the upbringing of their loveable granddaughter.

I make these observations because the 1960s were, without any doubt, a period of defining moments and social changes, even more so in 1967 when the bill to legalise abortion was passed in the House of Commons. This, together with the availability of the contraceptive pill, revolutionised the freedom of women to be able make their own choices in life.

As a footnote to the year, my scooter gave up on me. It desperately needed a new gearbox, but I had neither the inclination, desire nor money to have it repaired. In any event, my interests were rapidly moving on to changes in fashion, music and my life as a whole, which would in some measure define my future.

One of my favourite stores in Southampton was Tyrrell and Green. It was part of the up-market John Lewis chain of stores and was popular with me because it sold clothes which were very up to date and modish as well as the relatively expensive Nine Flags range of eau de toilettes, manufactured in the USA.

As a result of my frequent visits to the store early in the year, I noticed and got to know a girl named Jo, who was a consultant on the Lancôme cosmetics counter. As expected Jo, a brunette, was beautifully made-up, had a Mary Quant hairstyle, a seductive smile and wicked laugh. Her dress sense was pure mod. In my mind she was an altogether very attractive prospect for a date. The only drawback was that I heard that she was already committed to one of the mods forming part of the Concorde crowd to which I belonged. Not to be put off and full of determination I approached Jo's 'boyfriend' and asked if I could take her out. He said, with a knowing smile, that as I was part of the same crowd, he had no objection to this.

With what I perceived was a clear playing field, I approached Jo, told her that I would like to take her out and that her boyfriend did not mind. Somewhat startled, Jo burst out laughing saying that she did not presently have a boyfriend and yes, she would go out with me. I almost leapt over the building knowing that I was going to date one of the most well turned out mod girls in town!

After a significant dollop of Nine Flags eau-de-toilette and dressed to kill in my best mod suit, I met Jo in the centre of Southampton. She was absolutely stunning. Full of pride, I escorted her to the Concorde

Club where, upon our entrance, I was met with many compliments and winks from my mod chums, all of which made me feel a very lucky man. This was my first date with Jo and I wanted to impress her. Having found a seat I asked her what she wanted to drink. I thought it might be a port and lemon. Imagine how I looked when she delivered her response. The words brandy and Babycham stunned me. Fumbling in my pocket as if searching for a pot of gold, I could feel that this was going to be a very expensive night. Three more brandy and Babycham and that would be it. The date could turn into a disaster.

As it turned out, the evening was a great success. The so-called boyfriend was one of Jo's previous acquaintances and pretended still to be dating her, so as to deter others from trying to do so. He was there that evening. Jo and I bopped away, but spent most of the time talking so as to get to know each other. She was particularly interested in my career in law. At the end of the evening, I walked Jo to the railway station (she lived at Warsash, just outside Southampton) and we agreed to meet again the following week.

The following Saturday, we met at the cinema and had a meal in the Odeon Restaurant. The film was *The St. Valentine's Day Massacre* featuring Jason Robards as the famous gangster, Al Capone. A brilliant film enjoyed by both of us. The evening was another success and our relationship continued for the next two and a half months, following a similar pattern of clubbing, films (including *Bonnie and Clyde*) and restaurants. In fact, Jo had a likeness to Bonnie (Faye Dunaway)!

It was during this time that one of the mod fashions which emerged was modelled upon the twenties style adopted from films such as The *St. Valentine's Day Massacre*, *Bonnie and Clyde* and *The Untouchables*. The last of these was filmed as a TV series based upon the real Eliot Ness and his prohibition agents in the war against bootlegging and tax fraud in the USA during the 1930s.

Those films caused Paul and I to purchase suits in that style, consisting of double-breasted jackets with large lapels and baggy trousers, accompanied by two-tone brogue shoes. As it was still winter, I also bought a fashionable Parisienne three-quarter double breasted herring-bone tweed coat. Some of our mod crowd followed this trend, even to the point of wearing trilby hats, as worn by Elliot Ness. In this apparel, we cut a fine dash of modern vintage style, as a group of mods walking through the town.

As spring 1967 arrived and temperatures started to rise, there was a need for lighter clothing. In my case I purchased a blue denim Wrangler jacket and matching jeans, together with Ben Sherman shirts completed with Docksider shoes. In fact, as we edged towards the summer, during a trip to Notting Hill Market, I traded my madras jacket for a pair of fine suede ankle boots in red and green stripes. I also purchased a blouson Harrington jacket; this was created when Steve McQeen played a character named Harrington in a war film that year. In fact, I also changed my hairstyle to an American college cut in the style of McQeen.

At around this time, other developments, both home and abroad, were to take place based upon the many changes derived from the swinging sixties, as will become evident. On a personal level, this started with me standing down from the youth council. This did not however affect my ongoing work and interest as a committee member of the youth club or my voluntary work at the law centres.

Further, I had, by now, written a number of poems, two of which were entered into a national poetry competition. One of them *The Flower That Through The Earth Did Grow* received a silver award. Shortly after this two more of my poems, *The Visit* and *This Loving Prize* were published in the poetry magazine, *Enigma*. These successes spurred me on to further increase my interest in poetry, including the writing of it, for many more years.

In May I passed the first of my preliminary law exams. This enabled me to move on further to the next stage in my career, and required me to increase my studies and sit another three examinations, to become an associate of the institute. Upon reaching that level I could then apply to sit the final fellowship examinations, to enable me to become a qualified lawyer with letters after my name. It was going to be a long haul, but I was determined to do it. Interestingly, a number of my contemporaries fell by the wayside at the first hurdle and moved on to other careers unrelated to the law.

Peter, the mod, 1967

The summer of love

As spring moved towards summer, America witnessed one of the most dramatic changes when one hundred thousand young people gathered together in San Francisco, California. Such a gathering was unprecedented and triggered what became known as the Hippie Revolution and placed Timothy Leary's legendary phrase, 'turn on, tune in, drop out', into folklore.

Similar gatherings occurred across the USA, Canada and Europe, collectively creating a counterculture which espoused free love and peace resulting in the birth of the summer of love. As this rapidly spread around the world, hippies everywhere became known as 'flower children', whose anthem was *San Francisco (Be Sure To Wear Flowers in Your Hair)*, sung by Scott McKenzie. It contained the provocative phrase, 'There's a whole generation with a new explanation'. The song got to number one in the UK and Europe, thereby spreading public awareness of the hippy culture. The Angel of Pop was Roy Orbison whose tones of love flew to the heavens. In fact, I later became an avid fan of The Traveling Wilburys, a collection of other gods of pop music, namely George Harrison, Bob Dylan, Jeff Lynne and Tom Petty playing together. What a songfest!

The counterculture had its own newspaper, *The Oracle*, with a circulation of half a million. Words such as psychedelic, marijuana, psilocybin (magic mushrooms) and lysergic acid diethylamide (LSD) became popularised, particularly by Timothy Leary, who was a strong advocate of the recreational use of drugs. The use of LSD was widespread, particularly amongst well-known pop stars and bands, as a means of creativity, outside of reality.

There is no doubt in my mind that the hippy counterculture together with its powerful psychedelic imagery had an influence on The Beatles' ingenious ground breaking album *Sgt. Peppers Lonely Hearts Club Band*, released in the summer, followed by their *Magical Mystery Tour*

EP in December the same year. On the single front, Procol Harem issued their enigmatic *Whiter Shade of Pale* at about the same time as the Kinks' sociocultural anthem, *Waterloo Sunset*. All of these were classics evocative of the times and would influence the world of popular music and performers for many years to come. In fact, whenever I hear the Kinks' song now I am reminded of where I was and what I was doing when I first heard it. Fronted by the song writing genius, Ray Davies, they are still one of the best pop bands of all time.

The drug culture was never my scene and if I did inhale anything illegal, it was passively. However, my brother, Paul, with his friend, Ray, and maybe others, experimented with marijuana and, quite possibly, amphetamines such as purple hearts and black bombers. These were certainly the drugs of choice amongst my own circle of mods, who gathered at the bowling alley in Bitterne, frequently. They would tank up at the weekend with drugs and every time they hit the town, were stoned. In their own special ways each of these mods were real characters, who had ways of making any evening a great event, with no one coming to any real harm. Certainly there were no punch-ups between us. I remember one of our mods deciding to go in to the army as therapy for his drugs habit.

Tagged on to the summer of love, there seemed to be more parties to go to in the town than ever before. I and my friends made good use of them, some without an invitation. Again, without any trouble.

One big party was at a large four-bedroom house in Millbrook, Southampton, overlooking the docks. It was a warm summer's evening and I was invited by my brother Paul and his very dapper, but long-haired hippie friend, named Ray, who, it turned out, supplied Paul with his drugs. They were fully armed for the evening. Ray had an eye for the older woman and this one, who he knew, owned the house. We arrived late in the evening when the party was in full swing. The gardens were full of young people in all manner of dress or undress, either hippie, mod or bohemian, dancing and writhing against a backdrop of psychedelic music. The air outside and in the house was pungent with the essence of illicit substances and fragrant joss sticks, which after a while made you feel giddy and tranquil in turn. Inside the house were four rooms, barely lit, but full of people. One was for music and dancing and the others each for drugs, free love and refreshments including food and drinks. The atmosphere was totally exotic.

Paul and Ray quickly disappeared into the drugs' room whilst I made my way to the room with drinks. I was thirsty. We had brought two bottles of wine and a pack of beer with us and I seized upon a cool beer. All of a sudden, a familiar voice called out my name and I saw Lyn, a secretary who had recently joined our firm, making her way towards me with a glass of cider. She looked absolutely stunning with long blonde hair falling over her tanned shoulders and dressed in a richly-coloured kaftan. She had flowers all over herself.

"Hippy?" I questioned.

She smiled, "Part-time mod really," which somehow set the tone for the evening with my mod mohair suit. We eventually went to the drugs room (Lyn wanted a joint) and then danced the rest of the night away, eventually eating some food outside and drinking in the warm night air before I walked her home.

It transpired that Lyn had a place at one of the London art colleges to study design and had joined the firm to make some money during the summer holiday. Her father, who was a lecturer at Southampton University, knew John Griffin, hence the connection with Lyn. Interestingly, Lyn's sister was a ballerina with the Royal Ballet and they were shortly performing Tchaikovsky's Swan Lake at the Gaumont (now Mayflower) Theatre in Southampton. She asked if I would like to go with her, and, having never before seen a live ballet being performed, I accepted without hesitation.

I enjoyed the ballet immensely and after the performance I was invited back to her parents' house where they had prepared a late supper. Imagine my surprise when a short time later Lyn's sister arrived with two other ballerinas from the show we had just seen. A lively discussion about the performance ensued, encompassing Tchaikovsky's wonderful score and the omnipotence of Rudolph Nureyev. It was a truly cultured experience which I have treasured to this day.

After that Lyn and I dated for a short while, until she went off to college. I never saw her again but sometime later I saw her mother who said that Lyn had settled down with somebody else on her course and was very happy. I believe that her sister became a soloist with the Royal Ballet.

Before departing from the subject, Paul and I experienced an interesting twist on the perception of a hippy. It involved one of Paul's friends and a visit to the Alexandra Pub in Southampton for a drink. Paul's friend was dressed as a hippy with a kaftan and flowers in his hair whilst Paul and I were clearly dressed as mods. Upon ordering our drinks, the landlord refused to give a drink to our hippy friend because of the way he was dressed. We had never before experienced such discrimination. In answer to the landlord's words along the lines of 'I'm not serving the likes of you' our hippy friend simply said, "Peace man," and gave him an inverted V-sign. We said that if he was not prepared to serve our friend, we did not want anything and left. The times were certainly changing! We never went there again.

In contrast to all that was happening in the summer of love, the Middle East was in danger of imploding when the Six-Day War broke out between Israel, Egypt, Syria and Jordan. Israel was victorious, but for many years to come the Middle East would be a smouldering cauldron of unrest right up to the present day. As young men we seriously thought this was it and that Great Britain would be dragged into another conflict with us being conscripted into military service, but fortunately that did not happen. Just as well, because in September 1967 my world was shifting in different directions.

At the beginning of the month I moved to another law firm in Southampton called Page, Gulliford and Gregory. The reason for the change was not only to earn more money, but also to expand my knowledge to other areas of civil litigation. Up to now I had a working knowledge of contract disputes (including debt collection), and family law (including separation, divorce, maintenance and property disputes, adoption and child care). My mentor at PGG was Eric Sephton, a very experienced and well known lawyer, specialising in contentious and non-contentious insolvency law both for individuals and corporate entities, including partnerships.

During the Second World War, Eric was a sergeant major in the 8th Army who saw a lot of action in North Africa and southern Europe. His approach to the practice of law was therefore direct and concise and I was to learn a lot from him during my time with the firm. His training skills allowed me to broaden my knowledge and stood me in good stead for my future career in the law, particularly cases in the higher courts.

Just before my move to Page Gulliford, a young lady joined Stephens Locke and Abel as a secretary. She was attractive and her name was Lesley Archdeacon. After a short while I asked her out on a date. Lesley said that she was in a steady relationship and had been for some, but was happy to go out with me.

The date went well and I learnt from Lesley that she had an older sister named Gloria. At the end of the evening I accompanied Lesley home and somehow saw her sister, who I took to be Gloria, an attractive brunette, smiling at me. The smile was tantalisingly friendly and I was immediately captivated. Although I would see Lesley regularly in the office, we did not go out again. However I could not get Gloria out of my mind and eventually plucked up the courage to arrange a date with her through Lesley. Little did I know at the time that Gloria worked around the corner at Co-op Insurance as a clerk in the claims department and together with a friend had been following me into town at lunch-times and after work.

Little did I know that my life was going to change forever.

Part 7
Gloria Archdeacon — my first wife and mother of my daughters, Emma and Anna

Gloria

Gloria Catherine Archdeacon was born on 6th November 1947. She was the eldest daughter of Dennis and Joyce Archdeacon. Dennis was the company secretary (later finance director) of Red Funnel Ferries and Joyce was a teacher. Gloria's siblings were Lesley, Geoffrey and Marion in that order.

The family lived in a large detached house at Church Lane, Highfield, Southampton, near Southampton University. Highfield, in those days, was regarded as a very a prosperous suburb. Dennis and Joyce were members of a local tennis club and they played regularly each week. On the social scale they could be described as lower middle class.

Gloria was educated at Regents Park Girls Secondary School (where she obtained a GCE in domestic science). She played hockey for the school and was a strong competitive swimmer. She was also a member of the school drama group. One of her appearances was as a shabby, unruly pupil in *The Belles of St. Trinian*, a hilarious comedy of the outrageous behaviour of pupils at a fictitious girls' school and the questionable but comedic conduct of the teaching and other staff. A photograph of Gloria in torn stockings, dishevelled tunic, a trashed boater and a threatening hockey stick, supported by a withering grin exposing the loss of some teeth, sums up her stage character perfectly.

On that note and true to her own character, Gloria, at the age fifteen, gate-crashed The Beatles, when on tour, at their hotel in Bournemouth and managed to have her photograph taken with Ringo Starr, her idol, and Paul McCartney, as well as get their autographs and that of John Lennon.

In addition to that, Gloria succeeded, at various times, in obtaining the autographs of Dusty Springfield, Adam Faith and Herman's Hermits when they were on tour.

As I got to know her, it was clear that Gloria was an avid fan of the Beatles and Bob Dylan as evidenced by the number of records collected by her and pictures plastered around her bedroom walls.

I was not surprised that she was also a fan of Southampton Football Club, attending home games and getting to know some of the team, in particular Ron Davies and Dennis Hollywood. It would not be too long before she obtained more signatures, particularly on match programmes.

All of this conspired to give me an inkling of the single-minded and determined nature of Gloria's character, which I was to experience throughout my life with her. She was certainly very independent and a lovable and strong-willed woman who could see the bright side of life and treat adversity with a smile.

From the start and following our first date I knew that I wanted Gloria to be in my life for as long as possible. No longer did I just want a date that would fizzle out over the course of time. In Gloria's case I really wanted to get to know more of her.

To start with she was a classical mod girl with a Mary Quant hairstyle, wearing the latest clothes and accessories, including white boots, to go with them. She was so cool that I was very proud to be seen out with her, more than I ever did with anybody else before. I knew that I would have to give up some of the time I used to spend with the Concorde crowd, but that was going to be inevitable when a serious relationship was starting to develop, as in our case.

So it was that we became a serious item, dating at least three times a week and in between giving ourselves space to do other things, as I did with my brother Paul and our other friends.

We both enjoyed going to the cinema and it was during our early courtship that we went to see Stanley Kubrick's futuristic film *2001 A Space Odyssey*. The whole concept of the film (a long-distance exploration of the universe under the control of a computer named Hal) was so original and dramatically engaging I thought I need not concern myself with its menacing outcome so far away in time.

At the same time, Gloria continued seeing and going out with her girlfriends, the closest of whom were Sue Pallett, Jo Burlefinger and Sue Martin. Sue P. was one of Gloria's oldest friends and was to be the first to whom I was to be introduced together with her fiancé, Dave, with whom I was to build a great friendship in the future. Jo B. and Sue M. were mod friends with whom Gloria would spend summer holidays caravanning in places like Bournemouth. What they got up to I dare not think.

Sometime just before our first date, Gloria had left home. At the time she was dating a caretaker and found herself a flat near the Dell. By the time I took her out, Gloria had returned home.

As with any relationship, we introduced each other to our respective families. After this we were invited to dinner or lunch, although this was not on a regular basis. However, each of us got to know the other's family to the point when we might be invited to stay overnight at their respective houses. I quite enjoyed that, even if I had to sleep on the floor.

Over the course of time our feelings for each other grew stronger and stronger and I became aware that I had never been so happy as I was with Gloria. We shared the same interests in music, film, clubbing and eating out, all of which was binding us closer week after week.

Inevitably, our relationship became very much more intimate and I realised that we had reached the threshold where we would have to consider the future, knowing that if we went much further and it failed, for whatever reason, one or both of us might be hurt. I certainly did not want that to happen. We were three months into our relationship when I began to question whether I simply loved Gloria, or, more importantly, was in love with her. I needed some space to sort this out and after some discussion, which became quite distressing, I decided to part company. Not a particularly good time, as it was December and Christmas was looming.

After our parting, I dated a secretary from the office named Barbara, but it came to nothing and I was not in the mood for prolonging it. To be frank, without properly realising it, my feelings were elsewhere.

A true love story

Just before Christmas there was a heavy snowfall in Southampton and public transport came to a standstill. One evening when I was out, Gloria called at our house and left a Christmas present for me. My mother asked her to stay for a while but she declined. I was stunned emotionally by this gesture bearing in mind that Gloria had walked three miles through the snow from her home and back again. The least I could do was to reciprocate her gesture with a gift in return. Having obtained the gift I made arrangements to meet Gloria one evening at Woolworths in the town centre to give it to her. Our meeting was very emotional and I wished her well with a kiss. My brother, Paul, accompanied me, because we were going out that evening, and asked what that was all about. I asked what he meant and he said he could not understand why, having seen how Gloria and I were with each other, we had broken up. I pondered on that for quite a long time.

The New Year came and went and in January 1968 I celebrated my 20th birthday. I was no longer a teenager and started to realise that on my next birthday I would become an adult.

Over the next two months I spent most of my time clubbing and going to football matches with Paul and our friends. I was not short of female company, but I was in no mood for anything serious at that time. Furthermore, there had been no contact with Gloria since before Christmas. Something was agitating me but I could not understand what it was. Before long, two unexpected events would dramatically crystallise my feelings.

In the early spring, Dennis and Joyce Archdeacon called at our house on a Sunday lunchtime and asked if Gloria was with me. They said that she was apparently going out with somebody named Peter and thought that was me. I disavowed them of that and said I had not seen Gloria since before Christmas. After they left something was triggered inside me. I could not fathom whether it was concern or some latent form of jealousy.

Shortly after that, in the early spring evening, I was walking along Above Bar, Southampton on my way home from work when I spotted Gloria heading towards me from the opposite direction. My heart skipped a beat and as we approached each other it was evident from our smiles that we were happy to meet again.

After an exchange of pleasantries, I asked Gloria where she was going and she told me she had an evening job at the Wimpy Bar, waiting on tables, to make some money for a holiday in Spain with a girlfriend. I asked if she was dating anybody and she was. His name was Peter and he was a model. With no hesitation I said she was not from thereon!

With that Gloria burst out laughing with a look of incredulity on her face. She asked if I was serious and I said I was. She had to get on to work and asked me to meet her at the Wimpy at ten p.m. when she finished that night. I agreed and later that evening we met as arranged and over hamburgers had a long discussion about where we were going and decided to re-kindle our relationship. We both expressed our feelings and agreed to meet up again as soon as possible. I accompanied Gloria home and we ended the evening with a lingering kiss. She never went to Spain that year and never went out with Peter, the model, again.

Having resumed my relationship with Gloria I looked forward with relish to what the future might hold for both us together. Through our eyes we could see the spark between us.

The year 1968, saw a number of violent and disturbing episodes abroad. The Vietnam war rolled on in the USA, where there were regular anti-Vietnam war protests. In France there were student riots in the streets resulting in some of the students barricading themselves in the Sorbonne. In liberal Czechoslovakia, a member of the Communist Bloc in Europe, Alexander Dubcek created reforms in the Prague Spring which were considered a 'step too far' by Russia, leading to intervention with the arrival of Russian troops and tanks on the streets of Prague and elsewhere.

In April, Martin Luther King, who championed civil rights for black Americans, was assassinated, followed two months later by the assassination of Robert Kennedy, the brother of the late president, John Kennedy (his assassin was a Palestinian named Sirhan).

In Britain, the Tory politician, Enoch Powell, warned the country that there would be 'rivers foaming with blood' due to an enforced influx of Asians expelled from Kenya, together with others holding British passports and their dependants.

Ironically, The Beatles issued their *White Album* which contained the portentous song *Happiness Is A Warm Gun*, written by John Lennon. Karma was around the corner.

As the year moved on, Gloria and I became closer and closer in our relationship and attempted to see each other at every opportunity. In the course of so doing I gave up my position at the youth club and confined myself externally to my studies with law exams looming.

Socially, I got to know Gloria's girlfriends and their respective boyfriends to the extent that we would all travel regularly to places like Bournemouth or London for a fun day out. These friends remained a constant presence throughout our time together.

I remember one such occasion very clearly. On a hot summer's day, Gloria and I, together with Jo Burlefinger and her then boyfriend, travelled by train to London with a view to visiting the Kings Road, Chelsea and Battersea Funfair. At that time, the Kings Road was the Mecca of fashion and I was intent on buying the latest mod clothes and shoes. Its importance was reflected in the number of well-known fashion houses and the celebrities frequenting them. On this particular day we happened to see Stirling Moss, the racing driver, Kenny Lynch, a popular singer (who was driving a jet-black Mini GT motorcar with similarly coloured windows) and Twiggy, with her muse Justin de Villeneuve.

We were spoilt for choice and ventured into virtually every shop of interest to us, interspersed during the day, with visits to a couple cafés and a local bar. Shamelessly, in Ravel I blew a week's earnings on the most amazing Italian oxblood fringed leather slip-on shoes. These became the most popular shoes I had ever purchased, so much so, that upon returning home, I received numerous offers to buy them from some of my fellow mods. They were not for sale and I wore them for many years to come!

At the end of the afternoon and laden down with our purchases, we took the bus to Battersea and spent the rest of the day into the evening at the funfair. It was vast and we had a fantastic rollercoaster ride through the beautifully lit trees alongside the Thames. In the warmth, looking up to the endless ceiling of the stars, added to the magic of the moment. I also got my first taste of the well-known London delicacy and must-have, of cockles and mussels. Delicious!

We rounded off the day with a rush by bus to get the last train home, exhausted, but nonetheless very happy. The following day I had a bit of an ache in my wallet!

It was in that summer that I took the boldest step I had thus far ever taken in my life. Gloria and I were making our way by foot on a warm Saturday evening to a party in Bitterne. We somehow had a minor tiff over nothing particularly important, causing Gloria to walk on without me, when I uttered the momentous words, "I was going to ask you to become engaged to me."

With that Gloria spun round and asked, "What did you just say to me?" I immediately repeated the words whereupon she laughed, said, "Yes," and started to cry.

I embraced Gloria and firmly looking into her eyes said, "I really mean it."

With that we gave up the party and made our way to a local pub where we spent the best part of the evening. Gloria wanted me to ask her parents, which I did when I walked her home. They were delighted and we had a drink to celebrate the occasion. The following week I bought Gloria a red garnet engagement ring.

The next few weeks were a flurry of activity. Plans were made for the wedding date, venues for the ceremony and reception as well as the purchase of Gloria's wedding gown and making of the bridesmaids' dresses by her mother. My best man was to be Paul and the bridesmaids were Gloria's sisters, Lesley and Marion, and my sister, Catherine (who would then be three years old). There was much excitement over the next few months as the countdown to the wedding day gained momentum.

In that period, we celebrated Gloria's 21st Birthday on 6th November 1968, which meant she reached adulthood before me. We had a great party and much was made amongst our friends of our forthcoming marriage. By the time of Gloria's birthday, two of her closest friends, Sue Martin and Jo Burlefinger, had already got married, followed in the forthcoming new year by the marriage of her other close friend, Sue Pallett. We were all moving in the same direction and were able to share our experiences together throughout this whole period.

As with tradition, the brides' parents set about preparing the guest lists and selecting the menu for the reception, in consultation with my parents, Gloria and me.

As the new year unfolded I found myself preparing to celebrate another important event, my coming of age on 4th January 1969. My parents not only put on a party at our home, which was attended by a good number of Gloria's friends and mine together with some of my cousins, but they also gave me a gift for life in the form of a signet ring inscribed with my initials. This was then a very traditional gift and token in firm recognition of becoming an adult at twenty-one years of age. This would, in years to come, be changed to eighteen years, thereby signalling that the responsibilities attached to being an adult, such as voting, could be entrusted to a much younger, vibrant and more modern generation. I have always worn the signet ring in eternal remembrance of my beloved parents.

Some time ago I found my old 1960s leather wallet which contained some interesting items. These consisted of Gloria's parents' notice of our engagement and my notice of Gloria's coming of age in the *Daily Echo*. In the same wallet I found six Odeon cinema ticket stubs from films Gloria and I saw together at about this time in our relationship. These films ranged from *Doctor Zhivago* starring Omar Sharif and Julie Christie priced at 5/- (shillings, now 25p) and *Waterloo* starring Rod Steiger and Christopher Plummer priced at 9/- (shillings, now 45p). In addition, I found a ticket to the Lulu Christmas show at the Gaumont Theatre (now Mayflower Theatre) priced at £1.25 for front row seats. I remember distinctly the Lulu show because she came off stage and walked along the front seats singing to the audience in that row including Gloria and me. When she got to me, she stopped and sang the whole of her then hit song, *To Sir With Love* and when finishing, fixed me with a broad smile and a cheeky wink of the eye. I was all smiles and reduced to pulp!

As 1969 rolled on towards our wedding, we set about arranging our honeymoon and where we were going to live, as a newly-wed couple. The first of these was simple and we had no difficulty booking a week in a holiday apartment at Westward Ho! on the North Devon coast.

As to finding somewhere to live this was a little more difficult and time consuming, until we eventually found what we wanted. It was a first floor flat at a house in Newton Road, Bitterne Park. The landlord lived on the ground floor and gave us the impression he owned the whole house. After making our inspection we settled on a very small rent and set about decorating the first floor rooms. The reason the rent was cheap was because we did not have a bathroom. Furthermore, we had one outside toilet, shared with the landlord. Not a particularly a good arrangement, but at least when we shut our door we could be cosy in our first home which was very affordable.

Our parents expressed their concerns, but Gloria and I convinced them that we were happy and took up their invitations to have a shower or bath at their respective homes, as and when required. In order to placate them, we promised our parents that we would continue to look for a more comfortable home.

After *2001 a Space Odyssey*, man planted his boot mark on the moon with the words "That's one small step for man, one giant leap for mankind." It was in July 1969 when Dad wakened Mum, Paul and me to watch on TV the touching down of the lunar module and Neil Armstrong taking his first step on the moon with those words. The whole world was watching in awe of what the USA had achieved. For generations to come there was much hope for reaching out to the stars, to turn the non-fiction of Kubrick into real fiction. We are still waiting.

My first wedding

On 6th September 1969, Gloria and I got married at Highfield Church, Southampton followed by a reception in the adjoining church hall. It was a wonderful day with Paul, my best man, bringing out the laughter in his usual cheeky way. Catherine, our little sister, was one of the bridesmaids. After the ceremony and on a warm midnight we travelled by coach to our honeymoon destination, Westward Ho, Devon, arriving just as a beautiful dawn was breaking over the Bristol Channel. Halfway through our journey, Gloria and I were the only passengers on the coach and it seemed we were in a romantic film with the moonlight and stars chasing us to our future destiny. Love was in the air all week, walking along the shore and bathing in the warm waters around us. In such loving comfort Gloria and I both agreed to start a family as soon as possible.

Within two months of our wedding Gloria told me that she was pregnant. We were both so very happy with this news which lovingly strengthened our feelings for each other. The news was received by our families with both joy and an element of surprise. The only dissenter was my father who, without thinking it through, said he was ashamed of me. This was of course, rich, coming from him, bearing in mind that I was also a honeymoon baby in 1948! He soon mellowed.

Elsewhere, there was a feeling towards the end of the 1960s, notably called the 'crazy 60s' by Michael Caine, that a new modern world was looming round the corner. In fact, in 1969 it was the time of *Butch Cassidy and the Sundance Kid* and *Midnight Cowboy* in cinemas, the Beatle's *Abbey Road* Album coming out, Woodstock storming America along with the Chappaquiddick (Kennedy) affair and people saying, 'it's when the sixties lost their innocence'.

Part 8
A family born, a tearful loss and a new life with "Dadmum" — 1970 – 1979

A family born

On 1st January 1970 the age of majority was lowered from twenty-one to eighteen which was extolled as a triumph for youth and fresh ideas. Gone were the 1960s as evidenced most significantly by the break- up of The Beatles and all that followed to be overtaken by the emergence of glam-rock and the punk culture, amongst other things.

On the home front, Gloria and I were preparing for the birth of our first child in about June. This was moving quickly towards us and our need to find somewhere else to live was becoming desperate. We had looked at a number of prospective properties, including a council flat, but none were suitable. However, fate was about to play its hand in the most unusual circumstances and in a good way.

The senior partner at Page Gulliford, Richard Harding, called me into his office in April and enquired how things going in our efforts to find another home. When I appraised him of our looming dilemma Richard said that he could help us. He contacted a partner he knew at Whiteheads Estate Agents who had a two-bedroomed, top floor flat to let in Shirley, Southampton. The address was 35 Lumsden Avenue, a large semi-detached property built at the beginning of the century which had been divided into two flats on the top and ground floors, each with their own entrances within the front entrance hallway. Having viewed the flat, which had recently been modernised, we quickly moved in. Sighs of relief could be heard throughout our immediate families.

Shortly after, Gloria was taken to Victoria House Maternity Unit at Southampton General Hospital, where on 20th June, at about nine p.m., our first daughter, Emma Louise, was born. It was a warm sun-scorched summer's evening and although I missed the birth, Gloria having gone into premature labour, I was overwhelmed with emotion to find her holding our new-born baby in her arms. We both shed tears of unbelievable joy and happiness. Eventually, that happiness was shared with our families, including my father. After a few days of recovery we settled down for the first time as a family unit in our new home. The birth of Emma united Gloria and I even more in our feelings for each other.

Following this, Richard Harding told me that our previous landlord was illegally sub-letting his own tenancy to us at the Newton Road property and had been found out. The letting agents concerned were Whiteheads who, upon learning that I was employed by Richard, colluded with him in setting up the tenancy for us at Lumsden Avenue.

We soon got to know our neighbour in the flat below us, an elderly and delightful widow, named Mrs Morehouse, but were surprised to see that her flat had not been modernised in the same way as ours. For example, she still used an old-fashioned range for cooking and the access to her toilet was outside. She also had no proper bathroom. Mrs Morehouse told us that she had lived at the property since the 1930s and that she was very happy to continue doing so. Throughout the tenancy we got on very well with each other.

Before long I was sharing with Gloria the changing of nappies, bathing and feeding Emma (sometimes through the night) and, of course, the weekly shopping, all of which I took in my stride, as a proud husband and father. Without too much difficulty Emma soon settled down to all of these routines, including, to our relief, sleeping through the night.

At about this time, our friends, Sue and Dave Pallett's, first daughter, Debbie, was born and this common coincidence resulted in all of us meeting regularly either at each other's homes and sometimes in the New Forest, or sharing caravan holidays together on the Isle of Wight. I have wonderful memories of these moments, highlighted by Emma and Debbie at the seaside, playing in the sand.

Fortunately, Gloria was not only an excellent cook, but also an accomplished dressmaker and seamstress, with her own sewing machine, and throughout the early years, was able to economically produce a number of delightful homemade clothes for Emma. These were complemented with baby-clothes knitted by my mother on the one hand and on the other hand produced by Gloria's mother.

On the home front, the last major event occurring towards the year was Emma's christening in September, attended by both sides of our families and followed by a memorable party at our home.

Elsewhere in the world, sectarian unrest brewed in Northern Ireland resulting in violence and demonstrations which over the ensuing years would continue to be a deadly and unwelcome headline feature in the UK.

On a broader note, the first jumbo jet landed at Heathrow Airport, thereby opening up a new age of long haul, supersonic travel for the masses.

Finally, Margaret Thatcher was appointed as Secretary of State for Education and Science in the newly elected Tory government of Edward Heath, little knowing that she would eventually become a creative force in the political history of the world.

After the dawn of the New Year, 1971, Decimal Day was declared in February. This resulted in no more shillings, sixpences, pennies, half-pennies, farthings, florins or half-crowns which were replaced by the new decimal coins. By their very nature these took some time to get used to, particularly when making purchases. I remember my grandparents struggling with the changes in their otherwise regular shopping and commercial budgets, but in time they got used to it. Decimalisation was one of the first steps in preparation for closer ties with Europe.

Throughout 1971 plans were made for two family weddings later in the year; that of my brother, Paul, to Diana, and Gloria's sister, Lesley, to her fiancé, David Chainey, a refrigeration engineer in his father's business. David, although a Chainey, was not related to me. I found this quite odd as we were both born and bred in Southampton. It even perplexed my father because when he spoke some time later with David's father, Frank, at one of the family gatherings they both concluded that we were definitely not related, although I remained unconvinced. Lesley and David were to have two sons, Darren and Anton. To complete this side of the family Gloria's brother Geoff, who worked for Esso at Fawley, was later to marry Christine, a teacher, and would have a daughter, Amy and a son, Ashley, followed by Gloria's other sister, Marion, who with her partner, Steve, a plumber, would produce a son, Jordan. Jordan became a policeman.

Historically, the name Chainey was descended from the Normans in northern France, hence Normandy. They in turn were descended from the Vikings, or Norsemen, from Scandinavia. Following the Norman

Conquest in 1066 the first recorded origins of the name in England were ascribed to William de Chesney, a wealthy nobleman from Normandy. He was the keeper of Oxford Castle for King Stephen, the grandson of William the Conqueror. Since then the name has morphed into a number of different deviations. Whilst on the subject, I always wondered if Paul's ginger hair and light brown freckling were part of a Viking heritage.

In May 1971, I successfully completed my second preliminary law studies and examinations and became an Associate of the Institute of Legal Executives. This enabled me to start my studies to qualify as a Fellow of the Institute. Fellowship of the Institute was a qualification equal to a University Bachelor of Laws. The distinction between the two was that fellowship was a qualification that required studies at a college in the evenings and on occasions, day release, under the banner of 'Earn And Learn' as opposed to full time studies. In other words, I could be practising law under supervision with a law firm whilst at the same time studying academically for my exams. The fellowship law courses were very challenging, but I was determined to obtain the fellowship qualification, come what may.

At this time I qualified as a costs draftsman specializing in drawing up bills of cost in cases where there were costs orders both at my work or for other solicitors in court with a costs judge.

On one occasion I had a high-money case in the high court for my employers. It was so costly on the other side that the high court cost judge wanted to allow three days in court to deal with the costs. My professional opponent was the solicitor in the case but he was not a costs draftsman. On the first day he was struggling with me, having had a good amount of the costs they wanted, chopped off by the judge, after my arguments. On the second day the senior partner of my opponents arrived and the same happened, again after my arguments. On the third day there was no opponent, so the judge asked me to phone them. Nobody answered my call and the judge got on to finish the case that day.

I was keen to get as much experience in all aspects of civil litigation as I could and therefore, in September 1971, I left my employment with Page Gulliford (with gratitude for what I had achieved in furthering my career with them) and joined the law firm of Bryan Colenso. He was a well-known sole practitioner in Southampton and offered me the opportunity to expand my experience in every aspect of family law. This would give me a broader spread of knowledge to cover such matters as divorce, separation, child care (including adoption) and domestic financial and property disputes, together with all related contentious and ancillary matters, which amongst other things, might have to be determined by the family court as a last and/or necessary resort. This would also help me in my studies and exams.

Bryan Colenso (BC) was a bon vivant solicitor who had three sons, none of whom followed him into the law, much to his disappointment, and his elegant wife was the practice manager and cashier. I warmed to BC, not only as my employer and adroit lawyer, but as a raconteur telling me of his exploits as a pilot flying Lancaster Bombers during the Second World War. He also supported and encouraged me in my legal studies, including day release as and when required, and paid me a generous salary. Both he and his wife really did take a genuine interest in my young family.

Throughout my time with Bryan Colenso, Gloria would regularly make a trip into the centre of Southampton on Fridays with Emma for a lunchtime snack together. Every week I looked forward to spending time with my family. By this time Gloria had made a number of friendships with other mothers at frequent visits to post-natal classes, which was a very new and innovative practice put in place by the family clinics springing up at the time.

In consequence of these experiences, the birth of Emma and the whole concept of parenthood, Gloria and I made plans to expand our family further. In theory we tinkered with the idea of having four children in two year cycles. With the progress I was making in my burgeoning career we considered this to be economically viable and an exciting prospect. In short, this was one of our dreams for the future. Little did I know at that time what lay ahead.

After their wedding in September 1971 Paul and Diana came to live with us whilst they continued their search for somewhere else to live. After a short time they moved to a top floor flat in Upper Shirley. Although we were overcrowded and enjoyed their company we were glad that they were able to find somewhere so quickly.

The same year Rod Stewart released one of the most successful solo albums of all time. It was called *Every Picture Tells a Story*. It contained a number of unforgettable songs, most of which were written by Rod the Mod. The most memorable track was *Maggie May*. It was very innovative and as a composition, both musically and lyrically, set the trend for another style of popular music. In fact Rod Stewart was to go on and produce more great albums (including *Atlantic Crossing*) over the years which were to shape rock and roll and eventually propel him into the Rock and Roll Hall of Fame as one of the top five hundred recording artists of all time. Gloria and I were certainly great fans and I remain so to this day.

During 1971, the first British soldier was killed in Northern Ireland during sectarian violence between Protestants and Roman Catholics. As the year drew to a close the unrest in the province was about to get worse.

The year 1972 started with Britain joining the European Economic Community on 22nd January. Whilst there were some benefits in so doing, I felt that our sovereignty was at risk, particularly in relation to the functioning of our legal and court systems. This concern was to manifest itself in the following years through, for example, the European Court of Human Rights, particularly when Tony Blair's Labour government introduced into our law the Human Rights Act. It was, and still is my view, that this was the worst act of parliament ever made in our legal history, in that it weakened the social fabric of Britain and made our nation vulnerable to dangerous and malign forces. At the time I am writing this we are trying to leave the European Union.

The world on fire

Eight days after joining Europe, Britain was involved in one of the most violent events in its history. It occurred on a Sunday in Londonderry, Northern Ireland when British paratroopers, under attack by rioters, shot and killed thirteen people. 'Bloody Sunday', as it came to be known, was to haunt successive British governments forever after. The outcome of this tragedy was that the IRA embarked upon a concerted campaign of bombings, shootings and loss of life in Northern Ireland and mainland Britain for a number of years to come.

In addition to this, industrial unrest gripped the nation when miners went on strike, resulting in workers being laid off, reduced working hours being introduced by employers and regular blackouts following a shortage of coal stocks and electric power, which was due to the Tory government's shameful failure to properly address the issues involved.

I recall the blackouts at work and home and in particular a Sunday when our roast dinner was ruined following a power failure. We as a family, like many others, lived with candlelight and paraffin heaters for many days and nights during the following months. Without any doubt these were bleak times for the nation as a whole.

As if that wasn't enough, the Olympic Games in Munich were disrupted when a number of Israeli team members were taken hostage by Palestinian terrorists and killed in the resulting gun battle.

In the autumn, Gloria had a miscarriage and was admitted to Southampton General Hospital for dilation and curretage (D & C). Thankfully, the procedure would not affect her ability to have a baby and she was soon back home. We continued to look forward to a future with more children.

In January 1973 the Vietnam war between the USA and North Vietnam came to an end. It was a bloody conflict in which many lives were lost on both sides.

There was further unrest during the year both in Ireland and in mainland Britain, where the troubles continued, and the Middle East when Egypt and Syria attacked Israel in what became known as the Yom Kippur War.

The IRA at war in Southampton

I remember the IRA was a real threat locally on a number of fronts involving Southampton without the neighbours knowing it. Two suburbs in Southampton, Portswood and Millbrook, had active members of the IRA operating in their houses, in two particular cells. Early on a cold winter's morning a shootout took place in one of the houses in Portswood, between British security forces and IRA gunmen in a back street. This had the effect of bringing the centre of Southampton to a disruptive standstill. Furthermore, a raid by other members of the same security forces found in a number of garages at a council estate in Millbrook, an IRA arsenal of weapons and bomb-making equipment sufficient to cause significant damage and personal harm in mainland Britain on a grand scale. This arsenal had been shipped through Southampton Docks. You can understand our concerns as a family with children, bearing in mind that these events occurred within three miles of our home.

In the summer of 1973, we went as a family to one of the Isle of Wight festivals, accompanied by Gloria's sister Lesley, her husband, David, and their infant son, Darren. The day was a great success and I can honestly say that this was Emma's first open air concert. Unfortunately one of the headliners, a pop band called Hot Chocolate, had an amplifier meltdown towards the end of the show, much to the crowd's disappointment.

In September I joined another firm of solicitors called Shenton Pitt Walsh and Moss (SPWM), a real county firm in Winchester. This would entail me travelling by train to and from work each week. The reason for this change was twofold in that firstly I wanted to expand my experience in high court litigation and secondly, but sadly, because Bryan Colenso had been diagnosed with a terminal illness, which would have entailed him in either folding his practice or shelving it off to another firm of solicitors. The risk of an uncertain future was too great. Gloria supported me in this move, knowing it offered a number of opportunities to enhance and better our future, despite the daily train journeys.

My mentor in this new firm was Clifford Walsh, a fearsome litigator, who had started his career as a high court clerk to the senior judges and then qualified as a solicitor. His knowledge of high court practice and law was encyclopaedic and I began to acquire a significant taste for this more intellectual and challenging area of legal practice. At this time, I became a legal adviser at a community relations law centre, mainly helping people in difficulty with their lives.

And so it was that I entered 1973 with a new page in my career and the very welcome and exiting news that Gloria was pregnant, again.

It was the year when both Edward Heath, the Tory prime minister and Richard Nixon the American President were forced out of office; Heath after a general election and Nixon due to a Congressional loss of support.

On 14th May 1974, on a warm sunny evening, I was present at the birth of our second daughter, Anna Ruth. I cannot express my joy at watching Gloria giving birth to Anna. It was awesome and beautiful at the same time, rendering me speechless as our emotions overwhelmed both Gloria and me. It was quite dramatic because the midwife, who was a trainee, had just visited us on the ward and told us that it would be a little time yet. Just after she left the ward Gloria went into a strong contraction which resulted in Anna's head popping out. At that moment I shot out into the corridor and summoned the midwife back, by which time Anna had been fully born, on her own! The midwife placed Anna in my arms as she worked on the placenta. Interestingly, the young lady in the bed next to Gloria, together with her young man, were both transfixed in awe at what they had just witnessed!

Emma and Anna were christened with the second names of their great- grandmothers, Louise for Emma and Ruth for Anna. Throughout the ensuing months, we took the children to many trips out to places like the New Forest and the Isle of Wight in summertime, plus journeys to Wales with the whole family. It was a great time for everybody. Emma took to her new sister very quickly and wanted to help in caring for her, at such moments as Anna's bath time and breastfeed. On occasions, I would take both girls out to the nearby parks to give Gloria some time for respite.

During those months Gloria suffered from abdominal problems, which her GP put down as being a post-natal consequence following the birth. Following each visit, he would prescribe a white liquid for constipation which was totally ineffective.

Eventually, in October 1974, Gloria was seen by a locum doctor who carried out an internal examination. The result was bordering on the catastrophic, as after an immediate biopsy, Gloria was informed that she had cancer of the bowel. She was immediately taken into Southampton General Hospital where she underwent surgery.

During her recovery in hospital, Gloria received a large bouquet of flowers from the pop star, David Essex, who was performing at the Gaumont now Mayflower Theatre, in Southampton. It was our intention to buy tickets for the performance, but when her illness was diagnosed we had to put that on hold. To compensate for this, I contacted the local TV station on one of their interesting story programmes and appraised their presenter, Fred Dineage of Gloria's situation, after which the arrangements were made to deliver the bouquet. I had a lump in my throat when I saw Gloria's tearful reaction to this wonderful surprise. She was, of course, a fan of the star.

Following that in 1975, the parents on both sides paid for the two of us to have one week's holiday in Menorca. Gloria and I needed it and we had a good time.

For the next two years, Gloria handled her illness with great courage. At home we went on as before so that the children could keep their lifestyles stable. Towards the end of that period, she was told that she had secondary tumours in her liver and that her condition was inoperable. In other words her illness was terminal. The whole family was devastated, as were her close friends.

Despite this tragic news, Gloria faced it with great fortitude, dignity and strength of character in such a way that it touched all those around her.

In the period immediately before her death, Gloria and I tried to get on with our lives so as to cushion the effect of her illness upon Emma and Anna and to maintain a daily routine as normal as possible. This was assisted enormously by the loving care and warm comfort bestowed upon us by our very close families and friends.

During this time I passed my driving test at the first attempt and in consequence was given a second-hand Mini motor car as a gift from my employers. No more travelling to and from work by rail! The benefits of this were manifold.

In the summer, Mrs Morehouse moved out of the flat below us. That gave us an opportunity to ask the landlord if he would be prepared to sell 35 Lumsden Avenue to Gloria and me. I was told that he would for the sum of £6,000.00. Upon mentioning this to my employers they, through Gerald Moss, the managing partner, immediately set the wheels in motion to assist with the deposit of £600.00 (which we did not have, but was loaned to us by a client of the firm on very reasonable terms). Having secured that, Gerald referred me to John Dennis, the manager of Town and Country mortgage lenders, who after finalising the paperwork was able to give us our first mortgage, again on reasonable terms, to cover the balance of the purchase price and enable us to buy the property. Having completed the purchase and become proud homeowners, we set about engaging builders to assist with converting the two flats back to a four-bedroom house.

We had got to know our neighbours quite well by now and in particular became very friendly with John and Gloria Nightingale who purchased the house directly opposite ours. Their house was equally in need of renovation and John and I became involved in helping each other in some of the works to be done to our respective properties. John, a GP, and Gloria, a former nurse, had three children, two girls and a boy, the eldest of whom was Mandy. She was the same age as Emma. They became, and still are, life-long friends. Ironically, John was the locum doctor who conducted the internal examination which exposed Gloria's cancer.

Having restored our house, to the extent at that stage of only removing the partition segregating and opening up the two flats, we decided to have a celebratory party in December to which we invited a number of friends and members of the family. It was a great success and I was so proud to see Gloria enjoying herself as her old self again.

During the year another event occurred which could have changed our life in a way which I could not have envisaged, bearing in mind my background. I happened to notice in one of the legal journals, an advertisement for a civil litigator with an Anglo-American law practice in Bermuda. Tongue in cheek I applied for the job and surprisingly ended up being interviewed in London by the managing partner and the head of their litigation department, who was English. The managing partner was an American attorney with dual practice certificates in English and American law. Even more surprisingly, about three months later I received a telephone call from the managing partner telling me that I had been selected for the post. In consequence, he was going to arrange for me, together with Gloria, to visit Bermuda as his guest for a week. I was utterly stunned. The job offered a salary double to what I was currently earning and tax free with bonuses. I could see numerous opportunities opening before me and my family and for the next few days fell in to serious discussions with Gloria and our families.

The consequence of these discussions threw up two principal difficulties for us. Firstly, Gloria was still in recovery and receiving medication. Secondly and arising from this, the costs of any further treatment could be prohibitive, particularly if treatment for secondary tumours became necessary. I had appraised the Bermuda firm of Gloria's health and they were prepared to consider the position and how it might be dealt with.

Alas, after further consideration, I had to decline this very lucrative offer as the consequence of any further relapse was too risky. Furthermore, I would not feel comfortable in disturbing Emma and Anna's education if we had to return to England at short notice, if such a relapse should occur.

In the late spring and early summer we made separate visits to some of our friends, including trips to Wales and Guildford, which turned out to be very poignant, although I have to say that the journey in a small car laden with a family of four, tootling along the M4, was very daunting particularly when being overtaken by large articulated lorries.

The summer of 1976 was the hottest since the eighteenth century. Many people succumbed to the heat. Furthermore, we were deprived of making our very enjoyable and frequent trips to the New Forest either as a family or with friends, due to the risk of flash-fires, which could rapidly ignite and engulf large areas of the forest without warning.

In order to maintain Gloria's quality of life it was agreed that I and the girls should move in to live with Gloria's parents where she could be cared for by the family on a daily basis without unnecessary disturbance during her last few months.

Shortly before that Gloria, in a completely selfless act, asked me to purchase a number of ornamental roses, made of porcelain which she asked me to give to the closest of her girlfriends, after she had gone. In the regard with which Gloria was held, each of the roses were to be received with humility and great emotion.

Tragically, on the evening of 11th December 1976 Gloria passed away, surrounded by her immediate family. As she died, I caressed Gloria in my arms. The shock coursed through me and my grief was indescribable.

Alone, I stepped out into the early hours of the cold winter night. I shivered, both from the sharp force of the winter night and from the loss of my beloved wife. I walked under the street lamps for a while reminiscing about my short time with Gloria and quietly singing the Paul Simon song, *The Sound of Silence*.

As I continued walking my thoughts were temporarily interrupted by the sounds of voices, laughter and music of a nearby Christmas party. At that point, totally exhausted, I turned around and made the lonely walk back home.

The following morning, I took Emma and Anna for a short walk to the Southampton University campus. It was very quiet and empty. We sat down together and I gently told them of their mother's passing the night before. They knew that their mummy was unwell, l so I told them that she had gone on a long sleep at Christmas time and that we could talk about it some other time. I held back tears as I as saw a shadow of bewilderment and sadness move across Emma's face and heard Anna's request to go back home and see her Mummy. I gave them both a very gentle, warm hug.

Emma was six years old and Anna, only two. I was heartbroken. In the following years, Emma could remember her mother, but due to her age Anna could not. I therefore gave Anna photographs of her mother and her record albums plus other mementos, whilst I told stories of Gloria and what she was like. Amongst the photographs are pictures of their mother with Paul McCartney and Ringo Starr of The Beatles.

Gloria's family decided that it would not be prudent to take Emma and Anna to their mother's funeral. Their reasoning was to keep life going on as normal as possible. Gloria's ashes were scattered in a chosen place at Southampton Crematorium.

Following this, Christmas 1976 was naturally a difficult time, but it came and went as best it could, if only for the sake of Emma and Anna. Emma was at primary school and Anna being looked after by her grandparents. I would deliver Emma to school and Anna to my parents in the morning and then fetch both of them after work to take them home with me overnight.

With that in mind, I started to make plans to return to our home in Shirley. This was met with some resistance from Gloria's family, particularly Joyce, her mother, who understandably wanted the best they could offer in this respect. They postulated the idea that Lesley, Gloria's sister, should be a surrogate mother for Emma and Anna. Whilst not necessarily resisting this, I made it clear, that if life was to go on as normally as possible, both girls should be brought up by me, primarily as their father, in their own home. I made the point that it was too soon to make any other plans, particularly before the girls had been given the opportunity to settle into their own environment and way of life as motherless children. That said, I moved back to Lumsden Avenue with Emma and Anna during the latter part of the winter of 1977.

There is no doubt whatsoever that Emma and Anna gave me a strong reason to live and I soon realised that the responsibility of bringing up such young children, one an infant, counted much more than anything else in the years to come.

Furthermore I became acutely aware of the fact that Gloria and I had only known each other nine years and that her loss would change our lives completely. How I was to define that loss and my abiding love for Gloria would test me on a number of occasions during the years to come. In fact, for a number of years Gloria would return in my dreams and then she slowly faded away, leaving memories. I have two photographs of Gloria with Paul McCartney and Ringo Starr of The Beatles which I cherish with my heart.

Family law

During the period between 1973 and 1985 I developed a burgeoning family practice which I found very challenging and sobering, particularly when children were involved. Mainly, it embraced the breaking up of mothers and fathers and what would happen to their children and homes in the future after the breakage. Legal protection was needed when dealing with clients after a breakdown in their lives, both physically and mentally. As a family man I took it on with fortitude and understanding. It was something else I always wanted to take on in law when people in distress needed help. Before long I had a large practice, acting for more ladies than men, and through my secretary always with a box of tissues on my desk.

Much was needed to get the unhappy marriage into a plan of dignity to soften the sadness and pick up a recovery for the future. As a family lawyer in the courtroom, I did my very best to deal with the difficulties in order to get stability and the best results for my clients and their children as necessary.

Two suicides and a domestic murder

Sadly, there were tragedies. On two separate occasions my clients (both men) committed suicide because they thought they would never see their children any more after their divorces.

On another occasion I had a domestic murder case when my client (a wife) had a row with her husband as to who should slice the beef for Sunday lunch. The wife, with a carving knife in her hand wanted to do the cutting but the husband tried to snatch the knife from her. In a furious tussle with the knife in their hands the wife got it from her husband and plunged it into his stomach. The thrust of the knife was fatal. In fact, it was suggested in court that the death of the victim was caused by the removing of the knife from the body without any medical help. Murder is subject to the special defence of 'diminished responsibility' and at the following trial my client pleaded manslaughter to be settled on a mental detention assessment. Sadly, she and her husband were expecting friends for lunch and one of them removed the knife!

From the bench

There was the case of a famous Southampton football player and his wife who wanted to adopt a child. I was acting for them. When I got to the court, the judge called me into his chamber and I noted there was a social worker with him. He asked me if my clients' marriage was stable. Having said yes to the bench, he slipped a social report for me to see which said that the husband was having an affair (which I did not know) and he was therefore going to postpone the adoption for a year and that I was to tell my clients what had happened. In his chamber he said to me he was, "Bloody fed up, with young men like him with lots of money but no brain," and had a similar case the week before dealing with another footballer. Somehow, I was able to calmly tell the wife about the postponement through the social worker.

On two separate occasions, judges ordered me, through their clerks, to get out of bed to deal with breaches of non-molestation orders by husbands resulting in them each going to jail; the wives were my clients, one at Southampton and the other at Winchester.

Again when I was acting for a wife, she was having difficulties with her bullish husband about money divisions in their divorce. Having got nowhere, the irate husband bellowed, "And you can go and tell that to the fucking judge at Winchester!" Come the day, before the judge and during a cross question of the husband, he was asked what he had said to his wife about the judge in Winchester. In a very quiet court and with a waiting judge looking at him, the red-faced husband stumbled over his words. "Well, I didn't know the case was going to be heard in Winchester, did I?" to which the judge said, "And you didn't know I was going to be the "effing" judge, did you?"

In another case a judge asked a large docker, the husband of my client wife, how much money he took home each week. Being told, the judge said, "You earn much more than that because I have dockers in my court each week with money bulging in their pockets all the time, open yours." With that and while he was opening his pockets, he started a tirade against his wife in the court room shouting, "You wait when I get home." Having heard that, the judge told him he would be in prison shortly, upon which there was a great bang from the dock but no sight of the husband, who had fainted!

Elsewhere, the year ended with Margaret Thatcher having been elected as leader of the Conservative Party and the word 'punk' surfaced in the media for the first time in 1976. It was characterised by young people taking to the streets adorned with spiky or weird hair-dos of all colours as well as body piercings and with anarchic attitudes. The most outrageous punk band was the Sex Pistols, whose first record was inevitably called *Anarchy in the UK*. As with the 1960s, the scene was set for another explosion in youth culture and the world of popular music.

On a Saturday in the spring of the same year and against all odds, Southampton Football Club won the FA Cup against Manchester United at Wembley. We watched the game on TV and the following Sunday joined the crowds as the victorious team paraded the FA Cup through the streets of Southampton on an open-air bus. Driven by pride, there was a distinct party atmosphere on a grand scale in being able to witness such a rare and thrilling event.

At the beginning of 1977, Queen Elizabeth celebrated the twenty-fifth anniversary of her accession to the throne. In recognition of this very special milestone, the nation started to plan for numerous events leading up to and beyond the Queen's Silver Jubilee in June. Britain was united in celebrating the occasion, with all its pomp and glory, in the best way possible.

Equally, I was making plans for the future, including the upbringing of Emma and Anna and my ability to work full-time whilst continuing my external studies to qualify as a lawyer.

On the home front, Emma was already at primary school in Shirley and it was agreed that I would deliver her to school in the morning and that Joyce, Gloria's mother and thankfully a teacher, would collect her at the end of the school day. Having delivered Emma, I would then take Anna to be looked after by my parents. Upon my return from work I would collect the girls from their grandparents and take them home. This arrangement worked very well and I was eternally grateful to the grandparents for helping in this way.

As time went by, Emma, Anna and I settled into a regular routine of doing things together, such as preparing for school, assisting each other either at mealtimes or with homework, as well as each of us making up our own stories for bedtime. I mended the girls' clothes and altered their hemlines as necessary. We all got to know how to use the washing machine and cooker so that if any one of us had to do so we would be able to use them. All of these activities, which are not exhaustive, give some idea of the way in which we were bonding together as a motherless family unit. I wanted to ensure that our home was a place where we could have a lot fun together, given the circumstances.

Away from the home, we would, normally at weekends, venture to a play park or to the New Forest which was always a favourite. On frequent occasions we would visit the cinema to see the latest film, usually a cartoon. Whatever the event we might take along with us one of the girls' friends for company.

Within the neighbourhood, our house became a magnet for the girls' young friends to congregate on numerous occasions when they were not otherwise occupied. This brought me into close contact with their parents and enabled me to develop new friendships through a number of different social circles.

My closest neighbours were John and Gloria Nightingale and I was invited to a number of parties with them and their friends (who were mainly from the medical profession or local Catholic church).

It was through John and Gloria that I met their friend, Anja, a very attractive brunette. She was thirty-five, a qualified nurse and some-time air hostess, with Lufthansa (her father was German) whose late husband (a well-known South African cricketer playing with Hampshire) had passed away a year before Gloria.

Anja was also intelligent with a great sense of humour, although it was clear that she was still recovering from the tragic loss of her husband. We both recognised the vacuums created by the loss of our loved ones without dwelling too much on the sadness of our experiences. I particularly remember one evening following my return to Lumsden Avenue, and after the girls had gone to bed, when Anja turned up, unexpectedly, with a freshly-cooked paella, together with a bottle of wine. This took me completely by surprise, but, whilst totally speechless I was overjoyed to see her. Against the background of music from Rod Stewart's album *Atlantic Crossing* and a glowing fire, the meal and wine went down a treat, followed by a night of warmth.

We were an item for a few weeks after that and saw each other off and on throughout the spring until the start of summer. We then went our separate ways. At that time I was not ready for a long relationship or commitment.

A mist of grief

As the summer unfurled, I found myself in an emotional wilderness. It was manifested one sunny morning, just after I had delivered Anna to my parents for the day. As I was driving to work in Winchester I was suddenly overcome by a wave of uncontrollable grief. It hit me really hard. In the grip of this I had to pull my car over and stop immediately. I just could not stop crying. My whole body was convulsing and I feared that I would not be able to drive my car any further or go to work. As I slowly came to terms with what was happening, I suddenly found myself calming down and just as quickly as it happened, the grip on me was released. Later, I reasoned that it was the tortuous grief of losing Gloria which had lain dormant since her death until this moment. Whilst on occasion, I would continue shedding tears for her loss, the grip of such intense grief never visited me again. In fact, for many years to come I was haunted by dreams that Gloria had come back to me and that on occasions, disturbingly, I had re-married.

Whether or not the outpouring of such grief was responsible, along with Anja's brief relationship, I found myself in the summer of 1977 seeking the company of the fairer sex and embarked upon a number of short-lived relationships, some of which were intimate. It was as if women and their company were my drug. There was no shortage of them, whether at night clubs, parties (there were quite a few of these) or through friends, relatives and other acquaintances, and throughout this period my bed was seldom a lonely place. Some women wanted to get very close to me, but I was in no mood for a deep relationship, so soon after Gloria, who lingered long in my heart. I liked company, laughter and fun. I was lucky having my precious daughters Emma and Anna. They have been and will be my saviours for the rest of my life.

On my side in 1977, I got to a point towards the end of the summer when I started to question my lifestyle. It was all too easy to have one night stands with so many willing females, but I started to tire of them. I just wanted to slow down. After all, my primary responsibility was that of Emma and Anna and nobody else.

Furthermore, I was still working on the refurbishment of my house which, after my daughters, was a high priority. I had engaged builders to deal with the internal work, which was proceeding progressively, whilst I attended to the external work, ably assisted by a number of very willing friends. This was keeping me well occupied, along with my ongoing legal studies which were becoming more and more intense and time consuming.

As time moved on through the year and having reduced (and at times ignored) to a certain extent, my social life, I was introduced to somebody whose memory of that time stands out more than most of the others. Her name was Shirley.

My cousin, Tony, had recently remarried and his new wife had a sister, named Shirley, who lived in London. One day Tony telephoned and invited me to afternoon tea the following Saturday. He said that his sister-in-law was visiting and he thought I might like to meet her. As I was not dating any other person seriously at that time (apart from seeing Anja on and off as a friend) I accepted his invitation.

Upon arriving the following Saturday, I was welcomed at the door by a very stunning blonde lady with a beaming smile who said straight away, "You must be Peter, I'm Shirley." She led me to my cousin's dining room, where he was waiting with his wife, and he said "Your face is a picture!" and we all laughed. To say that I enjoyed the tea and meeting Shirley would be an understatement. I was totally smitten and wanted to see her again; quickly and as soon as possible. I felt totally uplifted in Shirley's presence. Just after I arrived at home after the tea, my head swirling with nothing but thoughts and images of Shirley, Tony telephoned and asked what I thought of her. I said that I was very keen to see her again. I asked Tony what she thought of me and he said "Phwoah!" loudly and promptly gave me her telephone number.

I saw Shirley again about two weeks later. She was spending the weekend with her sister. Having collected Shirley, we drove to a Greek restaurant for a meal on the Friday night. She told me she was a professional dancer and musician, having been educated at one of the dance and music schools in London. She also told me that she had a

Greek boyfriend who was also a dancer, but theirs was an on/off relationship, which was at the moment off. Shirley also told me that she had appeared in the film, *That'll Be The Day* starring David Essex. She was also a dancer, musician and singer on the Saturday TV shows. I was in thrall, of course.

The following day Shirley telephoned me and said she wanted to see me again that evening. We duly met up as arranged, the only difference being that at the end of the evening we spent the night together.

Over the ensuing months, Shirley and I met up as often as we could, bearing in mind her demanding showbiz commitments, during which time she got to know Emma and Anna quite well. She was great fun, always laughing and telling us of the well-known celebrities she had come across during her career. Alas, Shirley's career took her abroad and our meetings became very sporadic to the point when she was finding it difficult to continue seeing me. The last I saw of her was when she visited me one evening after many months away and informed me that she was going to Canada. We spent the night together for the last time and said our farewells the following morning.

My abiding memory of Shirley is that she injected into our lives an open heart no strings mentality which enabled me to involve her as another female with Emma and Anna, light-heartedly with no awkward questions. She was great fun.

As 1977 was coming to an end, we said farewell to the memory of The 'King', otherwise known as Elvis Presley, who died in August that year aged forty-two, two months after the Queen's Silver Jubilee (although a number of people were still convinced they had recently seen him in their local fish and chip shop!).

The next year, 1978, was fruitful on two accounts. Firstly, the refurbishment of my house was gaining momentum with the help of a couple of friends and builders, to the extent that new windows replaced the old at the back of the property, the kitchen and breakfast room were taking shape and central heating was installed throughout the building for the first time. To enable these works, Dave Pallett and I had to take down internally the chimney shafts on the ground and first floors to square off the rooms, a very messy job. On a Sunday we did that job, but totally damaged the old kitchen range. Having done the job, we each emerged from the house, coughing and spluttering, covered head to foot in brick dust and black soot, much to the hilarity of my neighbours. We laughed over a couple of beers!

Warren and Batchelor were a two-man local builder's firm, carrying out works on a property further up the road from me. One day they approached me when I was loading up a skip with debris. They introduced themselves and said that they had noticed me working hard on my property. They were apparently told that I was widowed and had two daughters, but that I had been working very hard on my property for some time, right into the evenings. At their suggestion, I showed them round my house and explained what work I had done and what further work was required. They were impressed and wanted to help me. I said that money was short and I could not really afford to employ them. They said that didn't matter.

The following day they turned up again and set out a plan for helping me with some of the heavier works on the house. These included windows to the back of the house and rendering the indoor walls where I had removed the now-defunct chimney shafts. They also pointed out the need to repair the ceilings. Money was of no concern to them at that stage and they were happy to talk about any payment upon completion of their work. Although I was concerned about payment, they were insistent on helping me. Within a short time they returned with the window frames and with a plasterer to do the walls and ceilings. They commenced work and completed it all within a week, including a glazier to finish the newly fitted windows.

I felt a great weight had been lifted from me and could not thank them enough. I had about £300 in savings and offered most of it to them. They demurred and suggested £100. I felt some embarrassment, but they said they were happy to leave it at that. That night I felt that some guardian angel had sent the builders to me.

Many years later I came across Batchelor (I cannot remember their first names) and he instantly recognised me. I was delighted to meet him and to thank him again for their generosity all those years ago. He told me that he was on his own now, still doing carpentry, but that Warren had joined the ambulance service.

A Fellow of the Institute

In 1978, and despite the pressures of the building works on my house amongst other things, I successfully passed my law examinations in the summer and qualified as a Fellow of the Institute of Legal Executives, with the letters F.Inst. Lex. after my name. In addition, I became a commissioner of oaths. This gave me a tremendous boost personally and also in my aspiration to become a higher court lawyer in civil litigation, ergo an advocate. As a proud father I recall tears falling on my cheeks as I hugged Emma and Anna, following my success, and in memory of their beloved mother, Gloria, who gave me great inspiration throughout my studies. I also qualified as a costs draftsman specializing in drawing up bills of costs for other solicitors. An order for costs made in proceedings for a winner which are payable but in question would have to be settled in court. I have done this at trial many times and won.

Not long after my Fellowship and qualification I was invited to the Southampton and District Annual Dinner Dance for solicitors, a somewhat closeted affair as I was about to find. When I entered the premises, a solicitor I knew well said curtly, "Where do you think you are going?" I immediately said that I was a guest, at which point my host, a well-known barrister, appeared and said to me in a whisper, "One for you and one for them." Over time and from some quarters there was an atmosphere of 'them and us', but I got on with the job. That was reflected in a letter to me dated 13th March 2000 from Richard Smith, senior partner of Paris Smith and Randall, in which he said, "I do not know how you chaps manage to get all these extra qualifications and keep a full case load going."

As time went on and I was getting busy, I was invited to be guest speaker at the United Kingdom Agricultural Seed Traders Association lunch on the topic 'enforcement of commercial contracts'. Throughout this I got a good idea of the difficulties some farmers might have in dealing with European contracts, in particular. There was a great debate and I took away many papers and thoughts which I found all very interesting, including polishing up my French.

During the year, my mother noticed that, whilst looking after Emma and Anna and with my head down in my studies and work on the property, I had not been on a date for some time. I told her I was devoted to my children and perfectly happy doing this. Wisely, she reminded me that one day the girls would each go their own way and that she would not like to see me left on my own.

I pondered on my mother's wisdom and decided one evening in the late summer to go to a discotheque on board a Blue Funnel Ferry sailing around the Isle-of-Wight. Why I chose to do this I do not know, but what followed was like something out of a film.

Chairman of the Institute of Legal Executives,
speaking at the annual dinner, 1984

Fun on the Blue Funnel Ferry

There I was standing alone with a pint of beer in my hand, tapping my foot to the sounds of music, when two rather gorgeous young ladies approached me. They were both dressed for the evening in black mini dresses showing off the most amazing legs. They asked if I was alone and I said I was, apart from my half-full glass of beer. They asked what I did for a living and I said, dustman. They said I did not speak like a dustman. I asked what a dustman spoke like and they fell about giggling. I thought I could have fun with these two clearly willing girls and did so, as we danced throughout the evening together.

At the end of the evening we disembarked and they asked if I would like to go with them to a disco called Turpins in Southampton. At this point we were all well-oiled. Of course, I did not want to disappoint and therefore joined them in the short journey by taxi to the disco. Things were almost sabotaged when the doorman at Turpins would not let me in because I was wearing jeans. My two female companions were having none of this and invited me to join them for the rest of the evening at their house in Lordshill, not far from where I lived. By this time it was well past midnight.

I settled down as they dispensed drinks and we started to familiarise ourselves with each other. I confessed my profession, which seemed to impress them, and they told me they were both stewardesses on the Cunard cruise ships, such as the Queen Elizabeth. They had seen the world and what it had to offer and regaled me with some very interesting stories arising from their adventures at numerous ports. They were, quite frankly, very entertaining in the most adult way.

One of them, a brunette, sat very close to me on their sofa whilst the other, a redhead, busied herself with the drinks, of which they seemed to have a plentiful supply. Well-tanked up as we were by now, the brunette came on to me quite heavily, whilst the redhead disappeared upstairs. I was enjoying myself immensely on the sofa, listening to music, Kate

Bush singing her hit song, *The Man With A Child In His Eyes*, when the redhead re-appeared from upstairs almost naked but for a little negligee, and exposing enough of herself to make any man in the world happy. Whilst the stage was clearly set for a threesome, something inside me resisted the temptation and, coughing and spluttering, I made a hasty retreat through the door. I can tell you the air was very warm that night!

And so to 1979. It was the year when the Ayatollah Khomeini returned to Iran (having sent the Shah of Persia into exile), Russia invaded Afghanistan, Lord Mountbatten was murdered by the IRA and Margaret Thatcher became Britain's first woman prime minister.

A testing time for lost Taffy

The tale of Taffy, a Welsh cob stallion, came out in the newspapers. His fame was at the centre of a breeding row between Mr Cole (Cole) and the ministry vet over his breeding qualifications and was facing a number of inspections. I was the lawyer acting for the ministry vet who said that Taffy's testicles did not match up and refused to register Taffy for breeding, so Cole obtained a court order to try and untangle the difficulty. Unfortunately, in an answer from Cole to me as to where Taffy was, he could not remember although he thought Taffy was roaming the Welsh countryside and nobody could find him.

The court order was the latest in a long line of legal wrangles over Taffy and after a while Cole claimed that the vet used a straight measure, rather than a piece of string. When a second test was taken, the difference shortened from two centimetres to half a centimetre. Cole then said, "But he's growing all the time, it's probably bigger than the other one now," when talking about the testicles, of course!

Taffy's previous owner sold him to Cole after Taffy failed a test, upon which he took him to Wales, where Taffy was protected from a subsequent Ministry of Agriculture order to castrate or slaughter him. Cole then had an inspection on Taffy in Wales and another ministry vet declared him perfect. Unfortunately, to make things worse, the previous owner had been taken to court for failing to slaughter Taffy.

The previous owner managed to get an absolute discharge from that case and then issued a writ against the first ministry vet my client, claiming negligence. Having untangled all the mess, I obtained a third inspection from the court and Taffy would have to be measured again. When I told the owner, he said that Taffy was loose on a Welsh common but he couldn't find him. When I told the vet a ministry spokesman said the castrate and slaughter order was still in force and the ministry 'would not interfere with any planned inspection'. After all that I was told the licence issued in Wales was not valid. What a sad tale indeed!

This was the year when following the help and assistance I received in renovating the outside of our house, I was able to make progress in completing the internal work. By this time, it had physically returned to being a four-bedroomed dwelling with a brand new kitchen and breakfast room plus central heating and other mod-cons throughout. Save for completion of some internal decoration, I was able to step back and admire what had been achieved during the last four years, since we bought the property. My only sadness was that Gloria was not around to share this with me. I consoled myself with the possibility that spiritually she was also sharing the moment. Spared of any further distractions I was now able to devote more time to Emma and Anna.

Furthermore and despite the turmoil of a domestic building site, we had, since 1977, shared a lot of time together holidaying in the Isle of Wight, particularly during the summer. I had found a very comfortable and family friendly guest house situated conveniently between Sandown and Shanklin. I can recall sharing the most wonderful times with the girls on the sandy and safe beaches between each of these resorts, come rain or shine. I remember carving out a large ship in the soggy sand for us all to play in, on a wet summer's day. Each of the resorts also boasted their own funfairs and promenades with cafés and seaside shops galore, selling fish and chips, ice cream and candy floss.

I would drive Emma and Anna to other attractions on the island such as Blackgang Chine, the dinosaur trail, Carisbrooke Castle, the Island Waxworks, the coloured sands at Alum Bay, Godshill Model Village and the Bird of Prey Experience at Haven Falconry. In short, we found we could find time to have fun as a good threesome throughout these motherless years. We are bonded together with love forever and they can openly discuss Gloria with me, always.

During the year, Anna joined Emma at Shirley School (in different classes) thereby making it easier for me to collect both of them from the Archdeacons after a day's work. Anna had formed a wonderful bond with my parents during the years they looked after her and she remained close to them for the remainder of their lives. I am eternally grateful to my parents for the help and loving care they gave to Anna at that difficult time.

Furthermore, both Emma and Anna started ballet classes with Pam Mandeville's School of Dance and Music. This opened up a new lease of life for both girls with an abundance of new friends and the opportunity of performing, not only in ballet competitions, but also on stage in musical shows each year. Such was the quality of the school that pupils were frequently taken up by the likes of the Royal School of Ballet and Ballet Rambert. It was not too long before Emma and Anna looked forward to their Saturday dance classes and socialising with their new-found friends.

Although I had two or three very short-lived relationships during the year, I was more than happy and content with getting on with my career and settling into the joyful contentment of family life with my daughters.

However, before the end of the year I came into contact with somebody who, in the future, was going to change our lives dramatically in a number of ways.

Part 9
Another decade, a second wife and more horizons on the future — 1980 – 1989

Beginning a new life

Early in January 1980, I met a young blonde lady named Sarah Taylor who was a secretary in another solicitor's office. She was nine years younger than me and I had seen her a number of times when I went to her office. She lived in Great Minster Street, Winchester. Eventually, we had a pleasant lunch and from that there was a year of what seemed to be contentment between us. From that I started a diary about our friendship.

Sarah's parents were doctors, Alan and Ann from Surrey. After a stint in Europe they had set up in America, with an Italian/American named Donald Panoz, a pharmaceuticals corporation based in the state of Georgia (the so-called deep south of the USA). Alan was president. Donald Panoz was an entrepreneur and developed the nicotine patch! I was shortly to have a good time with him in America.

At Easter, Sarah's family came to meet my family and, in the summer, we announced our engagement in the Times newspaper. The wedding was to be in August the next year.

Whilst these events were developing, much was happening with Emma and Anna. At the beginning of 1980 they were rehearsing their roles for the stage musical, *Oliver*, produced and directed by Pam Mandeville, their ballet teacher. Then a friend and employee of the John Lewis store (then Tyrell and Green,) got the girls to model children's clothes at the store's Annual Fashion Show. Later that year, both Emma and Anna took part in a ballet festival in Southampton, at which Emma was awarded with the Junior Progress Cup in ballet. Additionally, Emma started playing tennis with her grandparents.

A portent from The Beatle's *White Album*

On 8th December 1980 the world was shocked by the news that John Lennon of The Beatles had been shot and killed in New York. This was ten years after the breaking up of the band. His wife, Yoko, was with him after a recording session. Somebody outside his apartment building called out his name and as he turned in response he was hit by five bullets. Wounded badly, he made it to the office of Jay Hastings where he collapsed. His last words were, "I'm shot." Such was his stature as an accomplished singer/songwriter that his image would live forever bearing in mind one of his songs *Happy Xmas (War Is Over)*.

With these events behind us, 1981 was going to be memorable for a number of reasons.

The first was the appearance of Emma and Anna in Pam Mandeville's production of *The Wizard of Oz*, in which they played munchkins. The show was another success, resulting in both girls keeping their very colourful outfits. This inspired me to make Anna's seventh birthday a fancy--dress party. This theme was taken up wholeheartedly by Anna's guests and I turned up as a clown. Furthermore, at the show Pam Mandeville asked me to chaperone the Southampton and England Football star, Kevin Keegan, and another football player whose daughter was in the cast. Some show that was, for me as well!

With joy at the time, my second wedding was at St. Peter's Roman Catholic Church, Winchester (Sarah being a Roman Catholic) with Emma and Anna as bridesmaids. Our honeymoon was in southern Ireland for one week. While we were there Emma and Anna went on a week's holiday with their grandparents.

Incidentally, the royal wedding of Prince Charles to Lady Diana Spencer on 29th July at St. Paul's Cathedral, was watched by a worldwide audience of seven hundred million people!

Honeymoon in Ireland

After arriving in Ireland, we stayed in a guest house at Clonakilty in the south of Ireland. We took our car by ferry. This was at the time of the Troubles in Northern Ireland and I was informed before our departure that the IRA used stolen English cars as bombs in their armoury! Quite frankly, I found the Irish people to be very friendly with no hint of animosity towards the English whatsoever. On the contrary they were very warm-hearted, with a wicked sense of humour as evidenced by two visits I made, one to kiss the Blarney Stone and the other to drink Murphy's stout beer with the locals.

I went to see the site of John Mill's film, *Ryan's Daughter*, in which he gained an Academy Oscar, and then the beauty of Dingle Bay, including the long sands of Inch.

Displaying a mixture of curiosity and machismo I kissed the Blarney Stone. In so doing I found a very obliging Irishman with a wicked smile and hint of menace, tipping me upside down at a height of sixty feet. on a parapet asking, "Protestant or Roman Catholic?" I told him with a careful nervous, "Neither." Upon that and with a satisfied grin on his face, he blurted out, "You can kiss the stone now."

Upon our return home, we settled into the routine of family life again. In addition to their schooling, Emma and Anna were also getting ready and rehearsing for Pam Mandeville's next musical, *The King And I*, to be staged in the spring of 1982. They really enjoyed performing on the stage and were increasing their profiles with singing and speaking parts in addition to their dancing.

As a matter of fact, Pam asked me if I would like to play the part of the British ambassador, Sir Edward Ramsay, an offer I could not refuse. The girls and I had great fun learning our lines, songs and dance routines. These were precious moments in my time with Emma and Anna. When the show opened for three nights and afternoon matinees in April 1982, it was a great success (even though on one occasion I forgot my lines, which did not matter because the audience didn't notice!).

It was during this period that my brother, Paul, was going through a difficult divorce from his first wife, Diana. The sad fact was that Diana was adamant in moving to Shropshire to live with their two-year-old daughter, Gabrielle. This would obviously make it difficult for Paul to see Gabrielle regularly. After a while and with some determination from Paul, Diana relented and Paul was able to see Gabrielle on a regular basis and have her stay with him.

Kissing the Blarney Stone

War in the Falkland Islands

The most explosive event of 1982 was the Falkland Islands war in May with the United Kingdom. Hostilities started out with the ruling Argentinean junta seizing, by a military coup, the Falkland Islands in the South Atlantic, which were a protectorate of Great Britain. Although far away geographically, the unlawful seizure of the islands galvanised the British government, led by Margaret Thatcher, to protect the islanders and our territorial interests by immediately sending a task force, involving the three services, to regain them. Following a short but bloody conflict, costing the lives of two hundred and fifty-five British servicemen, Argentina surrendered.

This was then followed in July by the IRA bombing of Hyde Park and Regents Park in London, killing a number of soldiers and horses. This abhorrent and cowardly attack was one of the worst ever seen on the British mainland and shocked the nation, so soon after victory in the Falklands War. The government resolved to bring the perpetrators to justice and a long process doing so was put in hand, resulting eventually in a tenuous cease-fire.

The tragic sinking of the Royal Navy frigate, *Ardent* in San Carlos Bay by the Argentinian Air Force, reminded me that John Sephton, an officer killed on board the ship, was in the Scouts at the same time as me. Furthermore, his father, Eric Sephton had trained me at Page Gulliford.

Later, in 1987, I would meet Lieutenant Commander Tom Williams at a function in Winchester, who told me that he knew John Sephton as a fellow officer on the *Ardent* and that both officers remained at their stations when their ship went down. For his bravery, Tom was awarded the DSC.

Great Minster Street, Winchester, next door to Winchester Cathedral

In between these events we moved in to the house at Great Minster Street. It was a Queen Ann semi-detached house. Historically, it was the home of the Winchester Cathedral constable. This served us well for a number of good reasons. We now worked in the middle of Winchester and would have no transport problems for the four of us. Equally, Emma and Anna would be educated at Westgate and St. Bede Schools respectively. These both had good reputations and were within a short walking distance for the girls. Being in the town centre made it easy for all of us getting about comfortably. In setting up our future plans, I let Lumsden Avenue to my brother, Paul (after his divorce) and two young professional ladies, Claire and Dawn, as lodgers.

Backing onto the grounds of Winchester Cathedral, we had a grand panorama of the front of the church. Shortly after, we started to become acquainted with our neighbours in the street. They were a very interesting group of people.

Immediately, next door were Donald and Jean Judd who had moved to Winchester from London to live out their retirement. Donald had been senior partner of a firm of solicitors in the City and we soon found ourselves discussing a number of things in common. Jean had been Donald's personal assistant for many years. During our discussions I discovered that Donald had been a pilot in the Fleet Air Arm during the Second World War, flying dive bombers. They were initially the Albacore aircraft in the Western Desert and then the American Grumman Avengers in the Indian Ocean to support the British Pacific Fleet against the Japanese. He wrote his memoir, *Avenger From The Sky*, of which I have a signed copy. From this it is clear that Donald, whilst outwardly a very private man, bravely led his squadron on many dangerous missions, for which he was awarded the Distinguished Service Cross.

Directly opposite, lived Brian and Maureen Freemantle and their two daughters. Brian was a foreign editor with the *Daily Mail* newspaper and also a best-selling author of fictional espionage novels and non-fictional exposés of the CIA, KGB, world drugs trade and industrial espionage. It was said that Brian saved many people, some the last, from the evacuation of Saigon from the Viet Cong. On 31st April 1975 Saigon fell to the communist north Vietnamese forces. I had Brian as the guest speaker at one of the Round Table events. He was very well received! Maureen was a make-up artist for film and television. In addition, Brian's fictitious character, Charlie Muffin (from his novel *Charlie M*) was televised in the 1970s series of the same name, with David Hemmings in the lead role. Brian also told me that he had escaped a murder contract taken out by a Colombian drugs lord, interesting. I said to Brian, "I hope he doesn't knock the wrong door."

Living next door to Brian and Maureen were John and Sally Pruen. John had worked for the United Nations in Geneva and Sally was a Lebanese Palestinian. They were both long retired at the time I first met them and their son, Matthew. I believe that John may have been a contemporary of the coterie of poets at Cambridge. We had very interesting evening dinners on world affairs, including the everlasting cauldron in the Middle East.

On another occasion, at a noonday light lunch at the Judds home, Brian came dressed as a woman on the arm of John looking like one of the sisters from *Cinderella*. Over our gins, we couldn't stop laughing all afternoon.

This mixture of interesting people provided a kaleidoscope of enlightenment at cocktail parties which were a frequent occurrence during our time at Great Minster Street, but more later.

Having settled into these surroundings and the girls into their new schools, we flew in August to Georgia, USA for a holiday of three weeks. This would be my (and the girls') first trip to the USA and I was not going to be disappointed. America was vast!

The first of our family holidays in America

In the summer of 1982, we landed in the USA at Atlanta, Georgia through a white-knuckle storm and made our way by car with Sarah's mother and father to their home in Gainesville (the home of the author of *Gone with the Wind*). Little did I know that the next three weeks were going to provide me with some of the most memorable times of my life.

I noted that the mayor was a black American named Floyd Adams and that there were black American police officers patrolling the streets; thus I was seeing civil rights in action in the USA.

One of the striking features of Georgia was the red clay. It was everywhere. I recall this featured in one of the late Martin Luther King's speeches when he alluded to the freedom of 'the red hills of Georgia' during one of his civil rights marches. It was a spectacular feature which would throw up various hues of red during the heat and humidity of the day as the hot Georgia sun completed its move from dawn to twilight. As the day surrendered itself to the warm night the sonorous chirping of tree frogs took over.

After a couple of days' rest, we made our first trip out to the mining town of Dahlonega to pan for gold. This was the place where the first gold rush happened in Georgia in 1828. I quickly latched on to the fact that the gold miners of the nineteenth century must have been extremely patient in their quest for gold and, ergo, riches, as it took me hours to sieve out from the dirty water two to three miniscule pieces of gold dust which I hastily put into a small phial (which I still have). Small riches indeed, but great fun for all of us.

The remainder of our American holiday was spent as follows :

Driving to Gatlinburg, Tennessee through the Smokies, Blue Ridge Mountains and North Carolina. The forests and large expanses of fields with all their kaleidoscopic colours of flowers and birds were as good to see as a Disney film. In the distance we could see wild bears moving through the trees. Getting out of your car was forbidden.

Taking the world's largest cable car to the top of the mountains and back again with numerous people was huge fun, but in my case, I took a one-man luge to race the cable car back down the mountain at a great pace. Of course I won!

Going to a Cherokee show in the evening to watch an open-air play involving Native Americans entitled *Unto These Hills*, telling the true story of the upheaval of seventeen thousand Cherokees from their land in North Georgia to Oklahoma in 1838. This became known as the Trail of Tears, during which four thousand Cherokee perished. This was a very powerful and moving performance which depicted not only the infamy of the Cherokees being deprived of their homeland but also the refusal of President Jackson to execute the supreme court's finding that the removal was unconstitutional, in a case brought by the Cherokees. Having seen this and used the story in an earlier school essay, I felt very humble.

We climbed Clingman's Dome, which at 6643 feet, is the highest point in the Great Smokey Mountains. On my own, I went tubing along the Chattahoochee River in a leviathan inner tube from an inter-state articulated lorry, from Georgia to Alabama. What a bumpy ride from one side to the other. We took a trip through the swamps to see how White Lighting whisky was made by the Cajuns. Two of them gave me a bottle and informed me it was distilled through old car engines. I kept the whisky to give as liquor at dinner parties and, boy, it really was hot stuff. Later that day I played golf at Pine Isle with some bankers, losing ten balls. The Americans certainly did know their game and the pelicans followed us all round the course!

In the warm evening, there was a large barbecue where I was introduced to Donald Panoz, who took me for a moonlight ride in his shortened Cadillac Seville motor car, proudly fitted with a device he said neutralised speed cameras from the highway police! On return to the barbecue he told me he bought the car from Bob Hope, the American comedian and Hollywood actor.

Another interesting guest was a well-known American attorney named Chuck Blitzer who, the next day, took me to one of their large law academies at which I saw many old books and documents related to the American Independence and history showing many features of common law similar to ours. Chuck ended by saying, "Would you like to join us, Peter?" I was tempted!

The holiday ended with a visit to Disney World in Orlando, for a few days, where we stayed in the Contemporary Hotel. Emma and Anna had the times of their lives, and made diaries to show at each of their schools on their return.

Winchester Round Table

"Giving back to the community"

On my return from holiday, I was invited by a fellow lawyer, Nigel Ottley, to attend meetings at Winchester Round Table with a view to becoming a member. WRT was one of one thousand two hundred such clubs for young men in the UK between the ages of eighteen and forty, and thirty thousand worldwide. The Round Table movement was founded in 1927, the objective of which was to encourage fellowship between people engaged in their various occupations and to provide, through such contacts, service to the local community. The inspiration for this came about when the founder, on a visit to Winchester, saw King Arthur's Round Table hanging in the great hall. The motto of the movement was, and still is, 'Adopt, Adapt and Improve'.

At home, our move to Winchester in 1982 was going to provide us throughout the remainder of the decade with some of the best (and some trying) years of our lives, socially, professionally and educationally, which would touch upon and affect us all and individually as members of our family unit.

The year 1983 started in January with Anna taking up riding lessons with Goldfly Riding School which she would continue until 1987. During that period she also took up, through her school (following an attempt to play a trumpet), the violin (which she found difficult and gave up) and the saxophone, which she enjoyed, to the extent of joining the school orchestra. Emma continued with her tennis lessons and was eventually joined in these by Anna.

A tutor and actor

On my side, I started to deliver by invitation, tutorials on a regular basis to pre-examination law students at Fareham Tertiary College. This I did for quite some time to my benefit and to the benefit of the students mainly. That began my further future in the education of law students for a long time, both at my home and colleges.

Furthermore, I joined, by invitation from Alan Taylor, the St. Cross Drama Group, Winchester. He was a long-standing member of the group and a lawyer with SPWM. Following the usual audition, I was given two parts in Alan Ayckbourn's comedy, *Confusions*, delivered in four short stories about the stresses of middle class life. It was a classic of the author and a jolly good laugh.

Having thoroughly enjoyed this, I auditioned for the group's annual old time music hall, which resulted in me performing in a barber shop quartet, as the baritone and then as a soloist, performing one of the music hall's favourite songs, *Champagne Charley*. This was seen on one occasion by a John Stebbings, who played keyboard with his own combo. Amongst other things, the combo was a regular feature during lunchtime at Wisley Gardens in Surrey. This was largely attended by ladies of a certain vintage and good fortune, loosely known as the blue-rinse brigade. John seriously thought that having seen me performing I could be the next Frankie Vaughan and wanted me to perform with him at the gardens. Whilst I was very flattered by his confidence in my talent and much as I would have liked to try, I had to decline because I had enough on my plate at that time, due to my commitments with the amateur dramatics group and the fact I was about to become a full member of Winchester Round Table.

Performing with the St Cross Drama Group, Winchester, 1984

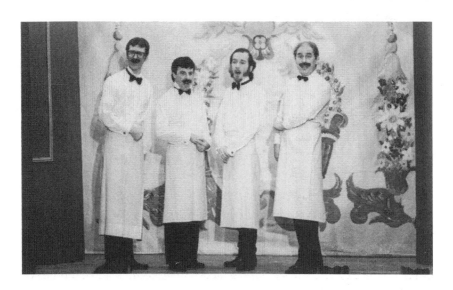

A knock on the door from an Ewok of *Star Wars* fame

As a commissioner of oaths I had a number of people coming in to my office to certify documents such as passports and immigration etc. One day, a man named Warwick Davis came to the office and there seemed to be some sort of excitement. My secretary came up to my room and told me Mr Davis was downstairs. I asked her to bring him up and she did, with delight on her face. I signed some papers for him and at that moment I knew who he was, an Ewok from *Star Wars*. We had a good chat and when I took him downstairs everybody wanted his autograph, including some clients. The month following, I saw him again to do the same business and that was it. He has, of course, gone on to greater things.

Lunch with a blonde bombshell from Hollywood

One opportunity which did come my way by surprise in February 1983, was an invitation from Isodan, one of my clients, to attend the launch of its new thermal insulation system over lunch at the Europa Hotel in Grosvenor Square, Mayfair, London. I had advised upon and prepared the franchise agreements for the client and the managing director wanted to show his gratitude for the work done by me. Upon arrival, I was told that I was to be a guest on the top table. Furthermore, I was asked by the MD to sit next to and entertain their guest of honour, who much to my surprise and delight was none other than Diana Dors, the very glamorous blonde film star, who was regarded as Britain's answer to Marilyn Monroe. To say this turned out to be one of the most memorable times of my life would be an understatement. She was not only larger than life in the flesh, but also great fun, very down to earth and easy to have a conversation with, despite her worldwide fame. I felt very humble when she voluntarily handed me a signed copy of the Luncheon menu addressed to Emma and Anna in whom she took great interest during our meal. I also reminded her that she owned a block of flats at Shirley, Southampton, something which generated great laughter of surprise. A small world indeed.

Diana Dors was born in 1931 and was an actress and singer from the London Academy of Music and Dramatic Art. In May 1956, she signed up to RKO Pictures and left Southampton on the *RMS Queen Elizabeth* for Hollywood. In August 1956, her film *The Unholy Wife*, came out in America where she was a great success. Certainly, with the American actor Rod Steiger. In Britain she was a blast on the BBC show *This is your life* in 1982. Sadly, on the 14th August 1984 Diana Dors died.

Friends from Australia

In November 1982 we had a visit from one of Sarah's school friends, also named Sarah, with her Australian husband, Alan, a geologist. They were on holiday and it was the first time Alan had come to England. He was especially keen to visit Stonehenge. On the third of November we made the journey to the pre-historic stones and I also showed Alan the remains of strategic scarp-top camps, burial mounds and flint mines, all of which he found awe-inspiring. Later in the day and after dinner Alan and I made our way round the pubs in Winchester and on our return were a little bit tipsy, and high in laughter.

In the summer of 1983, I sold Lumsden Avenue and with the proceeds of the sale, purchased not only a flat at Ashton House, Chilbolton Avenue, Winchester, but also my parents' council house, under the 'right to buy scheme', so as to secure their future. As to my parents' house, I made them the owners for the rest of their lives subject to a deed of trust in my favour.

Ashton House was a large Edwardian country house which had been divided into five large flats under long leaseholds. At the time of purchase, I also acquired the freehold of the property including some of the land for £1.00. Upon reviewing the freehold status of the property I discovered that I owned three large brick built sheds, which I sold a short time later to three of the tenants for more than £1,000.00 each. Not a bad return at all for £1.00. In addition to this, I realised that I owned, as freeholder, some of the land upon which the main house was built and which, upon enquiry of a chartered surveyor I knew, could potentially be utilised to accommodate twelve new flats, subject to planning. I kept this on hold for the future. We continued to live at Great Minster Street, whilst I let my flat at Ashdown House occasionally, and retained my interest in my parents' property to secure our futures.

At the request of Southampton University I gave two lectures, 'Cohabitation in the law and its effect on property' and 'A new education and training system in law studies'. This was all to bring up to date new changes in the law for first year students. Towards the end of the year, I started to expand my interest in the law by delivering tutorials at my home to final year law students in advance of their examinations in the new year. I did not take any money for this because I had benefitted from good mentoring in the past and I wanted to do the same for others in the future.

In the late summer of 1983, I became a member of Winchester Round Table. I had for some time attended meetings with Nigel Ottley and he proposed me to the table committee. After an interview with the membership sub-committee I was accepted. The induction ceremony consisted of me drinking a yard (two and a half pints) of beer in thirty seconds. I achieved part of this as best I could whilst the other part ended in saturating my shirt. Suffice to say my life was going to change significantly in the ensuing years of membership.

At the very beginning of 1984 I was still performing in the old time music hall and at the same time being appointed as chairman of the Southampton branch of the Institute of Legal Executives. Furthermore, as the year progressed, I was co-opted on to the committee of Winchester Chamber of Commerce with responsibility for publishing the chamber's magazine and organising the local schools' quiz.

Shortly after that, I was appointed fundraising chairman of Winchester Round Table, with responsibility for organising a number of fund-raising events, not the least of which was the traditional Winchester bonfire night on a Saturday in November each year. In addition to building the fire and assisting with preparation of the professional fireworks display, was included a candle-lit procession and carnival winding through the streets of the city up to Oram's Arbour at the top of the town. In advance of this, tablers had to go out in the evenings selling programmes advertising the event for charity. Our efforts invariably ensured that towards the end of the evenings we would congregate in one of the local pubs to down well-earned pints of beer and then go for a curry. On the next Sunday we set about sweeping up the mess and going to the pub again before going home for a well-earned Sunday roast.

Shortly after, I took up an invitation to join the new Winchester All Gentleman Golfing Society (WAGGS for short). I could not resist and accepted with glee. I had no doubt that 1984 was going to be a very busy year for me but I first had to get a decent set of Irons!

One Sunday in the summer I invited the mayor of Southampton to open a race for charity around Southampton Common between barristers, solicitors, legal executives and law students. We had many people turning up and all the lawyers made very generous donations to the mayor. For that I was invited by the mayor of Southampton to his next Christmas Ball as a guest on his table, with my wife.

That year Anna continued with her horse-riding and music whilst Emma (aged fouteen) hung out with her friends. At that time and in common with her schoolmates, Emma was in the process of choosing her options in readiness for GCSE examinations.

A second trip to America

During the Easter holiday, we made our second visit to the USA. On this occasion, we concentrated on making visits to the battlefields of the American Civil War, which took place between 1861 and 1865. It was of great interest to me, when I realised that the Confederate flag still flew in the southern states and that the conflict was still known by some southerners as the War Of Yankee Aggression.

Our journeys took us first from Savannah through Atlanta and right up to Washington DC, taking in the battlefields from Bull Run to Gettysburg. We then detoured to Harpers Ferry and past through the Shenandoah Valley incorporating another city called Winchester, in Virginia.

Whilst in Washington, we visited the cathedral (scene of Al Pacino's alibi at the gruesome ending of the great gangster film, *The Godfather*), the inspirational Lincoln Memorial, Capitol Hill near the White House, Arlington Cemetery, including the resting place of John F. Kennedy, lit in perpetuity, the Smithsonian and Space Museums and the Vietnam War Memorial, where I spoke with a couple of war veterans. I felt very humble when I was talking with them.

Towards the end of the holiday, we made our way to Savannah for a two night stay. I must confess to being overwhelmed by the beauty of the city, particularly the historical French Quarter and the traditional architecture of its balconied dwellings. It is no wonder, that when the Union General Sherman embarked upon his scorched earth march through the deep south, during which he totally destroyed Atlanta, but spared Savannah and made a gift of it to Abraham Lincoln. In doing this he emancipated the slaves. I noted that many southern men used the word 'yankee' rather than Union, for obvious reasons. The word yankee, is a derivative of the word English through the Iroquois, who, when meeting the English, said, "Yengis". We were the enemy in the civil war siding with the Confederates!

The journey to Savannah was through cotton fields and pecan trees, and was reminiscent of the film *Gone with the Wind*, which my mother saw many times in her life. Upon reaching the city, we were met with flocks of colourful mocking birds and cardinal birds.

As a family, we again had time to enjoy a great holiday, seeing so much more of America. For me, the Smithsonian and Space Museums (including Kitty Hawk) were a real blast. And then the many battlefields were awesome. Starting with Bull Run where the Union had to cross the Potomac River, Malvern Hill, the Battle of Shiloh, Stone's River, Chancellorsville and notably Gettysburg (more than four miles all round) to name just a few.

Before going home, I was given the gift of an entrance to the Augusta Masters Golf Tournament which I considered gold in sport.

Upon returning home, I set about preparing for a full calendar of all the functions I was to deal with and attend during my forthcoming year as chairman of Round Table. This started with organizing an open house as an all-day party at my house to raise funds for King Alfred Boys Club, of which I was also a committee member. Incidentally, Frankie Vaughan, the well-known crooner, was a patron and frequent visitor to the Club. This went on into the night, when we had a party for friends and neighbours.

This was then followed by the first ever duck dash in Winchester. This unique event entailed launching one thousand yellow plastic ducks to race down the River Itchen, numbered and subscribed for as a lottery, by members of the public. It was a great success for charity.

Towards Christmas, I suggested a used toys sale, with Father Christmas, to be held at the Winchester Boys Club. As an added feature I obtained the presence of characters from the popular *Dr Who* TV series, principally Mary Tamm (Alana) and Anthony Ainsley (the master) who were performing in a Christmas Pantomime locally. The sale was supported by our wives of the Ladies Circle who, on the same day, had organised a Christmas party for disabled children at the premises of IBM, Hursley. Both Mary and Anthony agreed to attend the party as an extra surprise, much to the delight of all who attended. What fun we had that day, particularly with our well-known guests, and the smiling faces of all the children and parents concerned. The stars put on a great show and some toy companies made donations of new toys from their stores for free.

As I was to set up the Chamber of Commerce Schools' Quiz after Christmas I obtained the services of Paddy Feeney, the well-known quizmaster from the TV and radio programmes, *Top of the Form*. His entertaining input ensured a full house and a highly enlightening level of knowledge amongst the young contestants taking part from each school around Winchester.

Running the schools' quiz, 1984

After both the toy sale and quiz, my wife and I had the pleasure of entertaining Mary, Anthony and Paddy at our house for supper, much to the delight of Emma and Anna who had some friends around to meet these well-known celebrities.

Each of these events were very successful and, including the annual bonfire night, raised more than £12,000 for charity during my year in office. I expressed special thanks to the Round Table team who worked hard to help me achieve such a good result.

Incidentally, I was able to capitalise on our success by hiring out our little yellow ducks to a number of other organisations for their own events, thereby ensuring a steady stream of income for charities throughout the years to come.

The year was capped by one further encounter which really did catch me by surprise and remains with me forever. It occurred at a cocktail party hosted by Brian and Maureen Freemantle at their home just after Christmas. In fact, due to the number of times we had cocktail parties each week over the time we lived at number two, I ended up calling our street Gin Alley.

Jane Austen's Mr Darcy in Great Minster Street

Upon arrival at the party, we were introduced to a number of guests, including some of our neighbours. After a while Matthew Pruen (the son of John), approached me with a tall young man with whom he had been at school in Winchester. There was a quick introduction and during my conversation with this young man he asked me what I did for a living. I told him I was a lawyer and in turn asked what he did. He said he was an actor and I immediately told him of my ongoing interests and performances with St. Cross Drama Group and the theatre as a whole. When I asked where and what his most recent performance had been, he remarked smoothly, "The Old Vic with Rupert Everett in *Another Country.*" Somewhat apprehensively, I looked up at the young man and asked him what his name was and he said Colin Firth. Our conversation continued animatedly, together with the drinking of gin martinis. A little time later Matthew gave me a gift *The Oxford Companion to the Theatre.* I treasure it as a reminder of my meeting with one of England's great actors.

The year 1985 started with my diary full of events and things to do, personally, socially and professionally. In fact it was going to be the busiest year of the decade.

To begin with, I left the firm of Shentons, having spent a number of happy years with them and built up a burgeoning family practice. It was time for a change. My next job, for which I was head-hunted by Martin Axtell, was with Bernard Chill and Axtell, a well-known litigation practice. My brief was to help to expand their personal injury department, particularly their steadily growing private client base of claims. I had known Martin Axtell, the senior partner, for many years and his approach to me arose out of a discussion I had with one of his colleagues at court who asked if I would be interested in joining them. I saw this as a golden opportunity to broaden my experience in another challenging field of law with a larger and totally different type of private client.

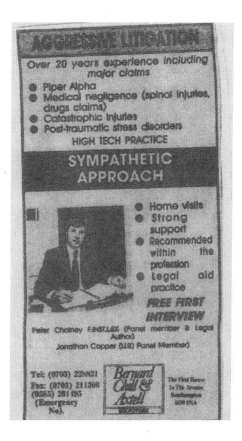

I had some experience of personal injury cases before and had an interest in the science and practice of treatments as shown in the magazine *Forensics and the Law*. The bulk and character of the injury cases being given to me were was going to be a challenge. I saw many of the trauma cases in the hospitals where my clients would be.

As time went by and I had a large number of cases in hand, the Law Society put me on their personal injury team. Furthermore, I became chairman of the local medical experts forum. This was to keep up with the movements of regulations between each of the professions including the hospitals. I also founded and chaired the Southampton Civil Litigation Group which ran very successfully for a number of years. At one meeting I had sixteen hospital consultants in my audience.

Due to my status, Bernard Chill and Axtell placed me in the press to outline their "Aggressive litigation — sympathetic approach" for difficult and major cases, such as Piper Alpha, catastrophic injuries and post-traumatic stress disorders. In dealing with these and over the years I got the names Terrier and Rottweiler from other lawyers and the judges due to me taking every point in a case to get a good result for my clients.

Allied to that and my chairmanship of the local branch of ILEx, I was invited to attend a number of professional dinners as a top-table guest. Some of these invitations brought me into contact with the likes of Enoch Powell, the Tory politician famed for his misunderstood, 'Rivers of blood', speech, and Sir John Donaldson, the Master of the Rolls, who was also head of the industrial court (a division of the high court), earlier disbanded in a flurry of bruising clashes with the trade unions. Both were very entertaining to hear.

The Right Honourable Lord Denning, 'the people's judge'

At the beginning of 1974 Peter Pitt, senior partner of Shenton Pitt Walsh and Moss, asked me to go to his room to help with two elderly gentlemen who had a family problem. Peter introduced them to me as Tom and his brother, Norman, friends of Peter. Norman had a married son living in Hong Kong with his Chinese wife and had a small child. The marriage had broken up and the son wanted to bring his child to England for a good education and, ergo, to live in Britain forever. Having thought for a while. I offered the options that may be available to the child without upsetting the difficult situation. The elderly gentlemen thanked me with handshakes and smiles as I left the room. A little later, Peter Pitt came into my room and said, "Well done, Peter, Tom, the Master of the Rolls, Lord Denning and his relative were happy with the way you handled the problem so succinctly."

On the 5th July 1985 I had a letter from the Rt. Hon. Lord Denning saying that he had "the greatest regard for all of you who are legal executives" and that he had 'always known… they were the mainstay of every firm of solicitors'. What an accolade from the highest judge in the land.

When I was in the High Courts of Justice in the Strand, London with a case, I noticed that Lord Denning was in one of the courts open to the public. With another lawyer we quietly entered and sat in the public benches. His lordship was with two other judges listening to an elderly lady who was obviously doing her own case without a lawyer. She knew a bit about the law and how to deliver her case to the judges. She went on for some time. What surprised me was that when she had finished every page in her book, she crumbled it up and threw the pages towards the judges, much to the chagrin of the court clerks but not his Lordship, who sat quietly. At the end of her case he smiled at the lady and said to her in his warm Hampshire brogue, "Is that the last of your ammunition?"

The whole of the court was stunned into silence. I will remember that scene for the rest of my life.

Also, in that year, Emma completed her education at Westgate School and moved up to Peter Symonds Sixth Form College, whilst Anna joined Queens Mead, a private school, to further her education. As it was summer, we went to Wales for a week and took the opportunity to visit Dylan Thomas' boathouse at Laugharne, Dyfed. Great for the girls because it was their third holiday to Wales which they always liked, for the large open spaces and long beaches.

Walking in the mist with Royal Marine commandos

One day I climbed the Brecon Beacons alone and as I was descending, late in the afternoon, I was engulfed in a dense cloud of mist and began to lose my bearings. I struggled to get through and started to call out for help because the cloud was getting darker. After a few minutes of near panic, I noticed something like an elephant coming down towards me. I noted that it was in a long line and immediately saw they were soldiers in battle kits. An officer and sergeant waved me over to join them. This I did and noticed they were Royal Marine commandos. I could hardly see their faces and none of them smiled at me. Eventually, we came out of the cloud on to a road, I watched the commandos march away in the same straight line until I could see them no longer. I was utterly proud of them.

Upon our return home I took a balloon ride, flying from Salisbury to Winchester, a very invigorating experience, especially when we were escorted at 1000 feet by two Microlights! The landing in a farmer's field was equally awesome as the basket carrying us hit the ground and was dragged for more than a hundred yards as the pilot deflated the enormous Balloon.

Following that, Paul, true to form, quietly married his second wife, another Diana (a social worker) and for a short time they took up temporary residence at Ashton House, whilst they completed the purchase of a property at West End, a village just outside Southampton. Bar one further short move around the corner, they would remain in that area until Paul's untimely death.

At about the same time, I appeared as the male lead in another play with Saint Cross Drama Group. It was called *Murder with Love*, a romantic thriller with a clever twist in the tail. I thoroughly enjoyed playing the lead, particularly when my leading lady became somewhat amorous in the love scenes.

The year 1986 started with Emma looking in earnest for a career upon conclusion of her academic studies and examinations. Meanwhile, she found temporary jobs with a delicatessen and then as deputy manager of Benetton, a fashionable Italian clothing outlet, both in Winchester. Whilst at Benetton one of Emma's customers was the Duchess of York. Eventually, Emma moved to London and became personal assistant to one of the partners in a city solicitors' firm, practising human rights law.

The same year, I was elected vice- chairman of Winchester Round Table and spent a significant amount of time supporting the current chairman and learning the ropes for my tenure as chair the following year, 1987.

In August we spent our family holiday in Normandy, France. As before, we camped and I was able to indulge myself in visiting those areas affected by the Second World War Normandy landings in June 1944. Whilst there was plenty of time for Emma and Anna to enjoy the beaches, we were equally able as a family to visit a number of historical places such as Pegasus Bridge and Sainte Mère-Eglise. This was the first time I had visited the area and I was to return many times in the years to come. As a result the Second World War has become a passionate hobby of mine.

In 1987 I became chairman of Winchester Round Table and was presented with a daunting calendar of Table events during my year in the chair. Included in the list of visits to other Round Tables in southern England was the annual debate, all in the cause of raising funds for charity.

I was up for this as a team member and I recall, on one occasion, we were to debate our proposal that 'the age of chivalry is not yet dead'. To flavour the debate with some light jollity, my theme was, that men should not break wind in the presence of ladies. For this I found the following little ditty:

Ode to a Fart

There is a gentle breeze
Which rises from the heart
And on its downward path
Is commonly called the fart.
The fart is very useful it gives
The belly ease, airs all
Dirty trousers and
Blows away the fleas!

Needless to say, men will be boys and with such rhetoric we carried the day into the next round, raising funds all the way.

On this type of subject, I had a case about a yacht. The owner said there was a problem about poor repairs work. At the end of the case I spoke to my professional opponent and asked him what the name of the yacht was. He informed me that it was FOWALUA. I asked him if it was Hawaiian. He laughed saying, "Rollocks, it means "F..k off world and leave us alone."

In the springtime, the head of Anna's school, Queens Mead, retired and the governors convened a meeting of the parents to make decisions for the future education of the pupils. There was some uncertainty amongst parents as to what was best for the ongoing education of the children, including Anna. It was decided that we would look elsewhere and were recommended Fernhill Manor Girls School in New Milton on the edge of the New Forest, close to the Solent. This was a private boarding and day school at which Martin Axtell's children had received their education and came highly recommended.

The big question was of course whether Anna was to be a day girl, Monday to Friday, or a full boarder, bearing in mind the direct rail-link to Winchester. I opted for the day girl option, but Sarah suggested boarding, because that would ensure a seamless week rather than disruption in relying upon the rail service on a daily basis, which could sometimes be unreliable. Despite my concerns, yet again, boarding it was to be for the next three years of Anna's education.

During the early days of her boarding I received a number of heart-wrenching telephone calls from a very unhappy Anna. At every opportunity, I would visit Anna until I finally fetched her home with great relief at the end her schooling in 1990. On reflection, I consider this to be one of the worst decisions of my life, bearing in mind what was to happen in the not too distant future.

Following my induction as chairman of Winchester Round Table I was quickly engaged in attending two very memorable events at the Guildhall, Winchester.

One was hosting a delegation of the fiftieth jubilee tour of Round Table, attended by many representatives from around the world. It was an astounding event bringing together many nations in the spirit of real friendship. There was much to talk about, with many languages, although most of the world could speak English The money collected on this tour went to charities worldwide.

Dancing on the frigate *HMS Alacrity*

The other was receiving an invitation to attend the officers' ladies night on board the Royal Navy frigate *HMS Alacrity* (the adopted ship of Winchester) at its berth in Plymouth. This came about when I attended, as a guest, the mayor-making ceremony at the Guildhall, during which I was introduced to Lieutenant Commander Tom Williams, the senior officer of the ship. We spent the evening together, during which Tom told me of the officers' ladies night on ship in May and that the tradition was to invite a civilian guest. Instead of the mayor, Tom invited me and my wife. We were delighted! On the night, my wife and I were billeted near the Wren's quarters at Tor Point and delivered by a naval limousine to the ship.

With the captain, on board *HMS Alacrity*, 1984

After dinner our wives or partners were taken to the wardroom for after dinner drinks, whilst the officers, including me, imbibed copious amounts of rum in the officers' mess. I must say that the carafe of rum seemed to be full each time it came round to me where my steward dutifully topped up my glass. Needless to say, that when we were called to the ward room to be reconciled with our other halves, we were well-oiled. The music started and we all got up to enjoy ourselves again with our wives. I recall that a few of the midshipmen remained in the officer's mess sound asleep with their heads on the table having enjoyed the rum. I danced with the captain in his officer's cummerbund which he kindly gave to me when we disembarked still singing away.

This, I can truly say, was one of the highlights of my life. It was made more pertinent for two reasons. Firstly, Tom Williams informed me, during one of our discussions, that he was involved in the Falklands War on board *HMS Ardent* (a sister frigate of *Alacrity*) when it was attacked and sunk by the Argentinian Air Force. Throughout his engagement with the enemy and in consequence of his part in the conflict Tom was awarded the Distinguished Service Cross. Secondly, Tom's number one officer on *Alacrity* was Lieutenant Commander Andre Usborne who was to become captain of the British Olympic bobsleigh team at Calgary Olympics 1988.

On a different level, in October 1987 the UK suffered one of the greatest storms during the night ever recorded, notwithstanding a reassuring weather forecast from Michael Fish, the weatherman at the BBC. There was devastation on a large scale when thousands of trees were blown down and many properties damaged. In addition, rail services were severely disrupted and traffic was virtually brought to a standstill due to the fallen trees. The damage took a long time to repair, at great cost, and in some cases the landscape was changed forever.

At the end of the year we made our last journey to the USA. This was to attend a family marriage, spend Christmas in America and make another trip to Disneyworld for Emma and Anna with Sarah's parents, leaving the two of us to spend time alone. Having settled down, our plans were almost immediately interrupted by two dramatic events.

The first occurred when, returning to the house following a day out, I noticed that one of the ground floor bedrooms had been broken into. I immediately telephoned the police who ordered us to vacate the property promptly, because the burglar might still be in it and would without doubt be armed. Within a short while, the police officers arrived. Having been given a sketchy layout of the house, they cocked their guns and moved off in different directions in search of the burglar. After a while they returned, and, having made a thorough search the officers gave us the all-clear with a caution to secure immediately the damaged bedroom door. Whilst I set about repairs, my wife telephoned her parents to let them know what had happened. Her father informed us that in their bedroom was a .38 handgun fully loaded and to keep it with us until they returned. There I was holding a fully loaded gun in my hand, waiting for Sarah's parents. I learned from this that firearms were a requisite for most American households.

The second event was something that was to catch the whole state of Georgia by surprise. It was struck by a very heavy snowfall. It was so heavy that it brought the entire state virtually to a standstill. In consequence we became housebound until it stopped snowing. This was the last week of our holiday and Emma and Anna were stranded in Disneyworld with my wife's parents. Two days before our return to England it stopped snowing and we monitored the situation in Georgia and Florida by telephone, in particular flights in and out of Orlando and Atlanta airports. Having learned the following day that both airports were operating a limited service, we made arrangements to travel by car to Atlanta. This was assisted by one of the close neighbours (who was in fact part Cherokee) who volunteered to deliver us in his Humvee Four-Track to the airport.

Upon arrival at the airport, we waited for Emma and Anna for some time and upon their arrival we were able to make our way to the departures lounge. There was a further delay due to only two runways being operational. Eventually we boarded our plane, a Boeing 747, and joined a queue of other aircraft waiting to take off. After four hours our plane rumbled down the runaway and raised its nose, heading for London.

Whilst the girls were away the mile-stone of my fortieth birthday came and went on 4th January 1988 without any notable celebration.

That was in some way salvaged when in March I hosted as chairman the Winchester Round Table Ladies Night and Jubilee Dinner. My guests were the president of Giessen Round Table (our German affiliate)

Herbert Zielinski, with a good number of his German members, His Honour Judge John Chalkley from the Winchester bench who was a past chairman of Andover Round Table, Tom Williams and Andre Usborne, supported by our wives and members from Ladies' Circle and Winchester 41 Club.

This was my last big event as chairman and it was a great success. In fact, John Chalkley, having seen Tom and Andre in full dress naval uniforms, remarked that if he had known it was going to be a ceremonial event, he would have worn his judges robes and wig. After dinner and in true round table fashion our German guests invited me to a drinking challenge with Schnapps. My memory is hazy but I gather from my guests that I drank well for Winchester. Herbert handed me a model Mercedes Benz 300 SL car made from the same metal of the real model. I have cherished this throughout my life with memories of my friendly European neighbours.

This event was to be my swansong because shortly after it I handed over the chairmanship of Winchester Round Table to my vice-chairman. As with tradition I was duly presented with the outgoing chairman's pewter beer mug, suitably engraved with the years of my chairmanship, and as a testimonial from my fellow tablers a wooden duck engraved with the words "In appreciation of a 'quacking" good year.' Furthermore, it would have been traditional for me to leave Round Table (as I had reached the retirement age of forty) and automatically become a member of the Winchester 41 Club. This I did, but in recognition of my time with Winchester Round Table I was also granted honorary membership for another year in Round Table.

As the year moved on, developments occurred which were going to have a far-reaching impact upon the future of our family unit. Emma was dating Matthew Thomas, the son of Leslie Thomas, the well-known author. In so doing, Emma met Terry Wogan and some other celebrities at the Thomas's house at Romsey. In addition Emma was invited to restaurants with Matthew and his parents, for a good while. She enjoyed the company of other celebrities during her courting.

Having started medico/legal work and become a specialist a number of major civil litigation cases came my way, which drew the attention of the public and media with great concern, shock and loss.

Chairman of Winchester Round Table, 1987

Piper Alpha — A tragedy that should not have happened, and the story of a hero named Stan

On the evening of 6th July 1988 a tragedy occurred on the Piper Alpha oil rig in the North Sea, which developed into the most disastrous event of its kind in modern history.

At about nine forty-five p.m. a condensate pump tripped activating the first-stage gas compressors and a flare was seen to be much larger than usual. Following that an explosion ripped through *Piper Alpha*. There was a high-pitched screeching noise followed by the flash and whoomph of an explosion. The first explosion caused a condensate line to be ruptured sending a second flash and bang, discharging a huge fireball roaring into the night sky. After twenty minutes a gas line, operated by Texaco, ruptured. Then after another thirty minutes a further gas line, operated by Total, ruptured, both sending gas through *Piper Alpha* at a rate of three tonnes per second. By the next morning *Piper Alpha* had been destroyed and lay tangled one hundred and forty metres below in the sea.

Catastrophically, there were two hundred and twenty-six people on the rig that evening and of those one hundred and sixty-seven perished, together with two crewmen from a rescue boat. Thirty bodies were never recovered, but sixty-one workers survived one of whom was Stan MacLeod a Diving Superintendent on the night.

Stan had a team of divers out and was at the sixty-eight feet decompression level on the rig. He was decompressing one diver when all hell broke loose around them in a shower of gas detritus, so he stayed with him. Notwithstanding what was going on around him Stan was able to save nineteen men on to the escape platform with Barry Barber, a diving consultant. This was all done under a ring of fire on the sea.

Lord Cullen held a Public Inquiry which took one hundred and eighty days. Despite several experts, many witnesses and survivors, it was not easy to know what caused the tragedy. Notwithstanding that, the inquiry concluded the likely cause was that 'a pressure safety valve had been removed as part of maintenance on the standby condensate pump'. Furthermore, Lord Cullen's report said, 'These personnel were efficiently and intelligently led and their orderly evacuation owes a lot to the presence of mind of Mr MacLeod and Mr Barber, the latter of whom perished when making his escape to sea'.

Stan came to see me to be his lawyer in the court case against Occidental in Edinburgh. There were going to be many other similar cases from around the world, including many lawyers and experts from engineering, gas and electricity cabling, shipping and marine structures at sea to name a few. I knew I would have to prioritise my case load. During that time I was making visits to Scotland and other venues, such as Birmingham, London, Edinburgh and Aberdeen to attend meetings, tribunals and court hearings to bring Stan's case to a satisfactory conclusion. The many showings of the destruction of *Piper Alpha* were horrendous to be seen in full.

During that time, a doctor in Edinburgh gave a me a room in his house overlooking the North Sea. It had a panoramic view. In the summer and after a long day of legal business in Scotland I went down to the sea for a swim to cleanse off my day. When I left Edinburgh, I would then go to see Stan at his house in the New Forest to keep him up with the case developments.

Occidental Petroleum (Caledonia) Ltd, the rig owners wanted to keep the legal jurisdiction in Louisiana for the case to be heard, but the English and Scottish lawyers were against that. This was because the Americans had a bad record for delay in payment of compensation through their appeals system. Therefore, after much pushing and hustling all around the UK, Occidental gave in and the lawyers (including me) agreed to a mid-Atlantic contract to hasten the pace for recovery and compensation with no more arguments. This became the biggest and most interesting case I had ever dealt with as a lawyer, in my life. The insured loss was £1.7 billion and the whole event was one of the worst man-made catastrophes ever. Stan was awarded the queens Gallantry medal for his bravery in saving so many lives, including those of his own divers. There is a memorial to the disaster at Hazlehead Park, Aberdeen, Scotland.

The first time I met Stan, we were both mods in the sixties. It was at the bowling alley, Bitterne where all the mods would assemble with their scooters and then spread out to Bournemouth, Portsmouth or Brighton for a day's riding. He told us he was a diver out of Portsmouth. After the *Piper Alpha* disaster, he felt he could not continue in that line of work and so he qualified in 1995 with an honours degree in osteopathy from the British School of Osteopathy London, initially in private practice. In 1997 he joined the NHS, specialising in neck and back pain at local hospitals. In 2000, he established a private practice in Fair Oak, Hampshire. On 23rd July 2003, Stan wrote to me saying he was currently employed by Southampton City Primary Care Trust and had a contract with the New Forest PCT. He gave me a batch of his calling cards which I put on my desk for clients.

The last time I saw Stan was at Chichester three years ago. He was one of the bravest men I have ever known and deserved his QGM medal from the queen. Under Scottish law the spouse and children would be compensated as well. Sadly, Stan MacLeod died on 28th May 2018 after a long illness. He was sixty-nine.

Hero who helped in Piper Alpha disaster dies at 69

by Stephen Walsh

11/06/2018, 8:10 am

Stan MacLeod, with moustache, meets the Queen. He has died aged 69

🖥 Send us a story

A Piper Alpha hero who helped save scores of men from the burning platform has died.

Stan MacLeod was awarded a Queen's Gallantry Medal for his efforts in helping to lead 19 men to safety after the North Sea structure exploded, leaving 167 men dead.

Mr Macleod, who was working as a diving superintendent on board the ill-fated platform, died on May 28 after battling a brain tumour for a number of years.

The 69-year-old was singled out for praise in Lord Cullen's report following his robust inquiry into the disaster, which made 106 recommendations for the industry.

Purley Station rail disaster

On Saturday 4th March 1989 in Croydon, London, in the early afternoon, a Littlehampton express train crashed into the rear of the Victoria express killing five people and injuring eighty-eight others. It was one of the worst accidents in the history of Network Rail trains. I had a client with injuries and from that I was brought in to deal with how the accident had happened. It was thought the collision was caused by one of the trains drivers going through a danger signal. The driver pleaded guilty to manslaughter and was sentenced to twelve months in prison.

However, the court of appeal ruled that the driver's conviction of manslaughter was 'unsafe because the infrastructure of that junction was causing mistakes to be made'. Furthermore, there was new evidence of 'four previous signals passed at danger at the same location'. The twelve months in prison was reduced to four months and then overturned in 2007.

This did not deprive those injured of their compensation and the Ministry of Transport report recommended that an automatic train protection system should be introduced without delay.

Benzodiazapine Litigation

Benzodiazapine was a tranquilliser with trade names such as Ativan, Valium and Librium and was widely prescribed from the 1960s for a variety medical conditions including anxiety, spasms, headaches, vertigo and insomnia. It was known as a drug of dependency and was addictive. In the 1980s it was becoming known that continuance of the drug was causing side-effects such as depression, fatigue, blurred vision and hallucinations. In fact, it could do damage to the brain and cause disabilities in babies born to addicted mothers.

I had a number of clients wanting to know how to deal with those problems. It was very difficult because my clients did not want to go to court for good reasons, such as lack of money, unless they could get Legal Aid. Added to that, the reputations of those in the medical world were being impacted. Nonetheless, I took up their cases. The benzodiazapine litigation cases as a whole created the largest class-action lawsuit in legal history, involving one thousand eight hundred law firms with me amongst them. The two defendant manufacturers were John Wyeth and Brother Ltd. for Ativan, and Roche Products Ltd. for Valium and Librium. In May 1988, a letter before action was sent to the first defendant and then a similar letter went to the second defendant in March 1989. In 1990 a judge of the high court started supervising the litigation.

There were more than twelve thousand plaintiffs (victims) on Legal Aid and five thousand started legal proceedings to test the water. Before long, problems were starting to surface when in 1992 the Legal Aid board initiated an audit to assess the viability of every case. In January 1993, Legal Aid funding was withdrawn from Roche cases and in February 1994, Legal Aid funding was taken away from the Wyeth cases. Further legal actions in the court, including those in the court of appeal, were struck out as an 'abuse of process'.

The woman in a Florida swamp

A little while after *Piper Alpha*, I was given another traumatic case, in which the media acted disgracefully. It started with a telephone call from Southampton General Hospital (SGH). It was from the neurological department and the manager asked if I could help with one of their patients they had just admitted. As chairman of the medical experts forum and a specialist lawyer in personal injury cases I was taken straight up to the department to meet a consultant neurologist, registrar, sister and manager. After introductions, I was given a patchy story of the patient and a summary of why she was in the hospital. There were many difficulties to sort out and the hospital gave the patient the name Nora.

The story was that a young nurse from Southampton was on a solo summer holiday in Florida, USA. At the end of the day she apparently went to a phone box to make a call home. It was dark and she was alone. The next morning she was found knocked out in a swamp with serious wounds to her head and still breathing. Two rednecks on a swamp boat had pulled her from the water. They immediately raised the alarm.

In a short time, the police and an ambulance had got Nora into a hospital in Florida. When stable, Nora was transferred to SGH in England for her recovery. Nora's head injuries were so life- threatening she would be in hospital, and then care, for some time. Meanwhile, I set up a power of attorney and registered it in the court of protection. From that time, and as I was an officer of the court, I gave recovery reports to the court regularly.

After that, I received a telephone call from the attorney general's office in Florida to tell me that Nora's assailant had been caught by the Florida police, was going up for trial and they would keep me informed. The charge was attempted murder, which may carry the death penalty in the state depending upon the recovery of Nora. At home, there was a frenzy of wanting to know amongst the press and other media, resorting to telephoning me and my brother (wrongly) asking, "Was she raped?"

The media were constantly telephoning me, and, on a number of occasions standing outside my office. If they caught me, I smiled and said, "No comment". To keep me informed, the hospital set up monthly meetings with me and all of those looking after Nora to exchange how far we were getting with her recovery. This included the court of protection and developments in America.

From the American side, I received a telephone call one day from the attorney general's office saying that the American people wished to help the recovery of Nora by setting up a fund. After consulting the court of protection and telling the neurological department at the hospital, the fund was set up. Amongst all of this Nora's consultant neurologist and I were watching the slow but careful advancement in her recovery.

The time came when the medics said Nora could leave the hospital and go into care. The best care for her was domestic, bearing in mind she was coming out of her teens. The social services team in the hospital quickly found a family at Lyndhurst in the New Forest with two children in Nora's age range. Following my last report to the court of protection, Nora went to live with the family. Five months later, I was invited to see Nora at the family home where she told me she had a boyfriend she had met at a night club and she was very happy.

After that, the American lawyers contacted me again to suggest that to avoid an appeal on the charge with a penalty of sixty years in jail we do a deal of forty years with no parole, to get it over. I agreed.

Following this I received, and accepted, an invitation from the board of governors at Lankhills School, a school for children with learning difficulties, to guide them through the requirements of the new Education Act. This act was very controversial in that it postulated the idea of taking children with special needs into mainstream schooling. This was naturally of great concern to the parents of children with learning difficulties.

In June I attended a Round Table convention of European tablers at Bezier in the south of France. This was, in fact, tagged on to a holiday at Bordeaux. We had all day to play games against other European tablers along the beach and in the evening, we had a large banquet in the grounds of a Mediaeval abbey right through to sunrise and breakfast the next day!

In August, Emma moved out of home to a flat with a couple of her friends in Winchester. I thought this was of her own volition and reminded her that she could always come back to live with us, which she did later.

In September we received some bad news. My father was diagnosed with cancer of the oesophagus and was told that if he did not undergo surgery immediately he would have only six months to live. It was obvious from this that surgery was the only option to him. This news caused tremendous distress to the family, with the prospect of a long period of recovery and the possibility that my father, at the age of sixty-four, might never work again (as was the case). Suffice to say the surgery was a great success enabling my father to live for another twenty-one years. The saving grace from this was that my father was able to enjoy his hobby of gardening and his allotments for the remainder of his life.

A divorce and the return home of my daughters

After nine years of marriage, I divorced my second wife on the grounds of her adultery. I was gutted and had had no previous inkling of her betrayal to me and my young daughters.

After the divorce, I continued to live at Great Minster Street until January 1991. During this time, Emma and Anna returned home to me. Anna started studying at Taunton's College, Southampton for a diploma in childcare. For the second time we became a motherless family unit, although the girls were by now grown up, more mature and moving on in their lives.

During 1990 and 1991, I was determined not to allow my life to stand still. I immediately took up playing snooker with Paul on a weekly basis and joined Winchester Tennis Club. For a short while I also took up playing racquetball. Later, I took up swimming which I now like immensely. Since my heart attack, I go to the gym and walk every day!

Eventually, I started dating again and came across a number of very agreeable and interesting ladies, including a belly-dancer. It was all very platonic and great fun, although at this time my emotions were not yet ready to be tested. That said, I must confess to having always enjoyed female company. This consisted mainly of taking trips to the local cinema and London to see a show, followed by dinner. I found this all relaxing as well as stimulating in soothing away the recent turmoil in my life. Thus, the time came when I was able to remove the cuckolded mantle of my life and move on with some more adventurous dating, but without strings.

With Anna

With Emma

Fun with the Australians again

A solicitor from Shentons, Nick Bell, was one of the first people who came to resurrect me from the darkness I suffered from my divorce. Nick invited me to a dinner at his home with some Australians from Rotaract, Perth. There were about eight men and two ladies. It was a blast! After we finished the meal the Aussies started a number of games, some of which were becoming a bit raucous. It eventually turned into a drinking game. Trying to drain the hosts' bottles from their cabinets, the Aussies started to stumble until I was left with one of the girls. She and I were quite sober, although I would not be capable of driving my car home. Therefore, we found ourselves talking through the night and didn't we do that. The young lady was a teacher and told me all about Australia. I was totally mesmerised. In a halo of the rising moon, she fell asleep on a sofa and I asked Nick to call me a cab, which he did, saying to come back later in the morning for coffee. Over breakfast, Nick told me the lady I was talking to was falling for me, but she had already left. The Australians really know their beers and how to live life with great amusement. I really liked those I met. I am a great fan of the Seekers and their rendition of *Waltzing Matilda*.

After joining the tennis club, a member named Sue, introduced me to a divorcee friend of hers named Chris who lived near Hythe. They had been nurses together. Chris was a health visitor, midwife and then a lecturer in midwifery in Brockenhurst, Hampshire. She had two delightful young sons, Christopher and Thomas. We hit it off immediately and for the next eighteen months spent a lot of time together, enjoying each other's company. This included weekly stopovers and holidays in France and Holland, some with the boys and all of which I thoroughly enjoyed. Chris and I were both in love and had a blast, but sadly not enough to go further than to the end of 1990.

In January 1991, I moved into a three-bedroom, end-terrace house at Swift Close, Badger Farm, Winchester with the proceeds of sale from my interest in Great Minster Street. Happily, Emma and Anna promptly moved in with me and we became a united family again.

Part 10
The Lady Next Door

An interesting neighbour

Throughout 1991, I started to take an interest in my next-door neighbour. How could I not do so? She was, after all, a striking and very attractive blonde. Although we occasionally exchanged friendly smiles and the occasional hello, we did not engage in any meaningful discussions, save for a brief enquiry as to whether or not I was the addressee on a postcard wrongly delivered to her. That said, I did note that she had many visitors, male and female, which suggested to me a very active social life. It was not until much later in the year that I introduced myself to her and learned that her name was Elizabeth.

Having broken the ice, I started to take much more interest in Elizabeth and exchange pleasantries on a regular basis. In fact, I did one weekend have a discussion with her father (who I did not know as such at that time) when he was mowing her lawn.

It was during this period that Elizabeth told me that she worked at IBM, Basingstoke. Furthermore, she told me that a work colleague, whose husband knew me from Round Table, told her that I was a barrister. This was of course not quite right and, for what it was worth, I told her of my correct position in the law.

Towards the end of 1991, I increased my focus more upon Elizabeth and took the bold step of inviting her to join me at my home for a drink one evening after work. Without hesitation she accepted my invitation.

During that evening, over a number of glasses of wine (a rather bland Liebfraumilch), I got to know quite a bit more about Elizabeth, not the least of which was that she was currently a divorcee and not in any serious relationship at the time. She also told me that she enjoyed having a full social life and was an avid traveller abroad. I found myself captivated and totally comfortable in the presence of Elizabeth, to the point where I did not want the evening to end. I had not felt so at ease for a long time.

It was shortly following this and, somewhat surprisingly, with the encouragement of my daughters, that I made my next move and invited Elizabeth out to dinner with me. She accepted, although I would have to wait about four weeks, due to her social calendar.

It was on 4th November 1991 that I took Elizabeth to an Italian restaurant in Southampton called Pinocchio's. This was our first date together and neither Elizabeth nor I knew then that this was going to be the start of something very special. I was mightily impressed, if not gobsmacked, when Elizabeth spoke Italian with the owner of the restaurant. From this I gleaned that Elizabeth had recently spent some significant time abroad at IBM's headquarters in Milan. I could feel that my interest in Elizabeth was growing stronger with every moment.

The year ended with a New Year party at my house attended by Emma and Anna, Paul and Diana and a number of friends, including Chris (who in fact invited herself). I went next door with the intention of inviting Elizabeth to join us, but could not receive any response to my knocking on her door. She told me later she was at another party that night.

The themed requirement of my party was a takeaway Chinese meal, to which all of my guests responded, and we ended up at midnight with leftovers of the meal singing *Auld Lang Syne* and doing the *Hokey-Cokey* outside in the cold of the night. At the end of the evening we all exchanged the usual wishes for a happy New Year little knowing that, in the case of my beloved brother, Paul, it would be the last one.

Before departing from 1991, there was one further event which occurred during the year and that was the publication of my first book by Blackstone Press Limited entitled *Legal Time Limits*. For some years in my career I had sent a number of articles which I had written as a correspondent, to legal magazines, all of which were published. That I was able to do this inspired me to write and publish my own book, something I always wanted to do. It was a practical paperback for the use of the legal profession, from students up to and including judges. I felt a surge of great pride and satisfaction when the first royalties' cheque arrived through the post.

New beginnings forever

On the 6th January 1992 I spent the evening having drinks to celebrate the New Year with Elizabeth at her home. I noticed for the first time that her style of home decorating was very unique and eye-catching artistically. It had a very warm and inviting feeling complemented by the sweet fragrance of joss sticks and, on this occasion, the haunting theme tune from the TV series *Twin Peaks*. I asked Elizabeth if she had been a hippy in the 60s and she responded that she was very much her own person when it came to trends both in fashion and interior decorating and, yes, she did tilt to that style and persuasion.

As the night unfolded, I found myself captivated by the genuine nature of Elizabeth, the way she spoke and her surroundings. At the end of the evening I was overcome by something special and was elated as we parted with a passionate kiss. As I returned home I had a strong, captivating feeling that it would not be long before we would embrace each other again. From then on, I was allowed to call her Lizzie.

My intuition was rewarded sooner than I thought when on 10th January I visited Lizzie again for drinks. This time I noted that we were becoming very relaxed in each other's company and I summoned up the courage to ask her if we could date on a regular basis. Elizabeth responded immediately and from then on we became an item.

Towards the end of January, I had an operation to remove a sub-mandibular stone from my jaw. Lizzie visited me in hospital and I realised from this experience that she had a very caring and tender nature. Upon my discharge she gave me two CDs, one by Scriabin and the other by Leonard Cohen. I knew little of their music, but over the years and nurtured by Elizabeth, I would grow and expand my collection of their work (particularly Leonard Cohen). And this was only the beginning.

In the ensuing years I would learn a lot from Lizzie about music and many other things which would embrace, strengthen and provide the solid foundations for a wonderful and very loving relationship.

Lizzie, a beauty in waiting

Lizzie Gay Brenner was born a Virgo on 17th September 1950. She was the first child of Lois Joiner (nee Kennedy) born on 17th October 1921 and Geoffrey Toodgood Stedman Joiner born on 25th February 1916. The father of Lois, William Kennedy, was a Scot who saw action as a captain with the Kings Own Scottish Borderers in the First World War. He unfortunately suffered a bullet through his foot and contracted gangrene, resulting in amputation of his foot. Throughout the rest of his life he walked with a wooden foot.

Both Lois and Geoffrey were called up during the Second World War. Lois joined the ATS, stationed in the north of England and Geoffrey was a driver with the Eighth Army Royal Artillery, seeing action in North Africa and Italy including the battle of Monte Cassino. In 1944/5 Geoffrey kept a diary of his push up through Italy with the British Army and I have this. Sadly, Geoffrey died on 14th May 2019 at the grand age of one hundred and three.

The second child (and brother to Lizzie) was Andrew Nicholas "Nick" Joiner born on 24th January 1954. The family home was Knowle, near Solihull. The immediate family was expanded when Nick married Joanna Beach and they had two sons named Patrick and Sam. Lizzie was educated at Tudor Grange Grammar School, having passed the eleven plus exam. Her further education was completed at Hall Green Technical College, and later in life, Leeds University

Eventually, Lizzie, after a stint of owning her own restaurant with her first husband, Laurence, in Harrogate, joined IBM, Birmingham and remained with that company until 1993. After divorcing Laurence, Lizzie married a second husband who also worked with IBM. That marriage also came to an end. As my relationship with Lizzie gained momentum, a number of events occurred during 1992 which rolled over into 1993 and beyond.

IBM was at that time one of the sponsors of Disneyland at Paris in France and Lizzie had an opportunity to visit this with some guests. She invited not only me, but also Anna and her boyfriend, Lee. We had a great time. In fact, Lizzie and I decided that if this visit was successful, we would live together, such were our feelings for each other. Accordingly, on 2nd April 1992 I moved in to live next door with Lizzie. I had discussed this arrangement with Emma and Anna who had met Lizzie on a number of occasions. Around this time Lizzie met my brother, Paul and his wife, Diana, firstly over dinner at a local Indian restaurant and then at Anna's eighteenth birthday party. Paul was immediately taken with Lizzie (particularly her Italian style of clothes from her time in Milan), but, unfortunately, tragedy was to strike. Two weeks after Anna's party, Paul died. Lizzie and I have often reflected over the years since, that we would have probably spent so many wonderful times together with Paul and his wife, but for this tragic loss. That Lizzie was there to support me in that dark time of my life was a miracle which, amongst other things, would unite us in love forever.

Time moved on and in the summer of 1992 Lizzie and I had our second holiday abroad together in Morocco. This was a well-earned break and just the tonic for both of us to make clear plans for our futures together. We discovered that we both enjoyed travelling and over the following years we would visit many destinations including Malta, India, Italy (including Sicily, Sardinia and the Amalfi coast) as well as France (many times, sometimes with friends there).

Furthermore, Lizzie had for many years visited Regents Park open air theatre with friends and in 1992, took me along for the first time. I was also hooked and we would, for many years thereafter, continue to attend performances of William Shakespeare and many other playwrights in the warm balmy atmosphere of a summers' evening, complemented by a pre-show picnic and copious amounts of champagne.

We particularly enjoy live concerts (popular and classical including operas and ballets) and mainstream, foreign and art house films at the cinema. In fact, I joined Winchester Film Society with Lizzie, who had been a member for years. Thereafter, we became members of Harbour Lights Picture House at Southampton and continue to attend this on a regular basis every month.

Through the medium of live performances, I have become a fan of Leonard Cohen, the legendary poet and song-writer, and Bill Wyman's Rhythm Kings. In fact, Lizzie has been an avid fan of Leonard Cohen from early in her life and has introduced me not only to his music and records, but also literature in the form of novels such as *The Favourite Game* and *Beautiful Losers* and poetry in his collection *Book of Longing*, all of which are very inspirational. We saw Leonard Cohen perform three times, including his last performance in Bournemouth

Having, fallen deeply in love with Lizzie, I presented her with an engagement ring on the 25 December 1992. A little while later, our wedding day was set for July 1993.

Three weddings and a wife for life

The year 1993 was full of hope and expectation for the future and particularly for our families.

Plans were afoot for two family weddings, that is mine to Lizzie and that of Anna to Lee. The logistics were planned, including the registry office, Winchester as the venue of choice in both cases and guest lists were drawn up.

Lizzie and I chose Pinocchio's restaurant for our reception, partially in remembrance of our first date. Quite frankly, we have always been very fond of good Italian food and for the ensuing years visited the restaurant until it closed. Interestingly, Raoul, the proprietor was a champion poker player and toured the world, including Las Vegas, regularly each year following the closure of his catering business.

Against this background, Lizzie and I took a holiday in the two weeks before our wedding in the Italian town of Amalfi. It was one of the most romantic holidays I can ever remember and provided the ideal build up to our wedding. Four of the highlights of this unique holiday consisted of visits to the Isle of Capri (where we visited the hotel in which Greta Garbo, the famous Hollywood film star, sought sanctuary from the pressures of fame and Hollywood in the 1930s and 40s), the extensive and awesome mummified ruins of Pompeii, a climb to the top of Mount Vesuvius, and finally to Ravello for an open air classical concert by members of the English Royal Academy of Music against the backdrop of the setting sun over Italy and the Mediteranean Sea. Ravello was, of course, the place where D. H. Lawrence finalised his controversial novel, *Lady Chatterley's Lover*.

The date of our wedding was 30th July 1993 (a date to remember). It was attended by our parents, Emma and Anna and some close friends. After the wedding ceremony and reception, Lizzie and I spent the wedding night at the Royal Hotel in Bath followed by a few days browsing around this delightful Georgian town. It was intimately exquisite, very romantic and memorable forever.

Peter and Lizzie's wedding, 30th July 1993

Shortly after our return, I had the great pleasure of hosting Anna's wedding to Lee, the reception of which took place at the Stanmore Hotel in Winchester, following a registry office ceremony. Whilst the actual event was a very happy affair, two developments occurred arising from it.

Firstly, my relationship with Gloria's family faded almost immediately into the mists of time, so that I no longer had anything further to do with them. I realised I was moving on in my life in a direction which was inevitably not going to involve them anymore. Anna was moving on in her life and four years later Emma would be going in the same direction after her own wedding.

Despite this, I encouraged both Emma and Anna to continue maintaining contact with their late mother's family, as I had done rigorously following her passing. To their credit, Emma and Anna, in their maturity, have each maintained a healthy relationship with that side of their family to this day.

Secondly, Anna was happy for a number of years, producing two daughters, Katie and Holly, but, alas, her marriage did not last. Eventually, Anna married again and with her new husband, Mark, delivered another daughter, Evie.

As for Emma, she got married to Ben in 1997. It was a novel ceremony, starting with the wedding vows being taken at the well-known Chelsea registry office, against the background of the song *Wonderwall*, recorded by the then very popular rock band Oasis. This was followed by the reception at the Duke of Argyll Pub, Covent Garden. In a somewhat laid back, smart casual way, there was a sit-down meal followed by a disco in the evening. As well as me supplying drinks, including champagne, the speeches were delivered by me and the newly-wed Ben. It all went well and was a lovely day.

After a while, Emma and Ben moved from Islington and set up home in Winchester. Over the course of time, two further granddaughters were delivered to my collection, named Calliope and Daisy. This meant that I was surrounded by females (of which I was proud), but found myself as the last living male on the line of my father's side of the family.

In November 1995, I created and set up Southampton Civil Litigation Practitioners Group after a meeting with the local judges. The group was open to civil litigators including barristers, solicitors and legal executives. This had the support of the circuit and district bench and I set up a programme of business meetings for speakers including judges, barristers and experts such as doctors and other professions. I was made chairman and group organiser of Law Society accredited seminars. In addition, I delivered a monthly newsletter to keep members, including judges and the courts, up-to-date as to what was going on in the law of civil litigation. I was the founder/chairman for ten years.

In March 2000, and after success in studies at London and Manchester Universities, I became a chartered legal executive advocate for the higher courts in dispute resolution cases, mainly in litigation. This was similar to being a specialist barrister in the court room. At last, my lifetime ambition had been achieved by going up the long and winding road with 'mud on my boots'.

Following that, in 2003 Richard Smith, the senior partner of Paris Smith Solicitors, offered me a post in their dispute resolution department covering every aspect of commercial and other disputes including corporate fraud, intellectual property, building/construction, professional negligence, defamation, land law and personal injury.

On 12th October 2003 an article in the *Independent* newspaper carried the headline 'The Top Brass... 10 leading legal executives'. Further, Sir John Harvey-Jones stated, "Legal executives are lawyers who progressed up their career ladder with mud on their boots." I was one of those ten lawyers and said, as a chartered legal executive advocate, "You can only get out of the law what you put into it. This involves hard work, a genuine interest in your fellow human beings and the awesome responsibility of knowing you can make a difference to people's lives."

An evening of sportsmanship

In 2006, Fairbridge Solent a charity in Southampton supporting inner city youth and of which I had been a member for some time, wanted to make a start on their annual event for charity. After some thinking I suggested an evening of sportsmanship at St. Mary's Stadium, home of the Saints, Southampton Football club. Fairbridge asked me to go ahead and do it.

It was agreed we have Allan Lamb as our celebrity speaker and maybe another. Allan Lamb was a South African cricketer who first played first-class cricket for Western Province and then Northamptonshire. He then was a fixture of the England middle order and was named Wisden Cricketer of the year in 1981. Retired, he went as good bat on the celebrity circuit. I also managed to get Mike Wedderburn of Sky Sports News as our presenter.

There was a large banquet for many companies and other people plus auctions after desserts. Money was coming down like rain. When dinner was finished there was a gratefully received surprise at the entrance of the footballer Matt Le Tissier of Southampton FC and England fame. From that time on, Mike Webberburn conducted an evening of sportsmanship between Allan and Matt and then questions from the floor. At the end of the event there was a swarm of people waiting for autographs. It was a great night and collected £8000 for Fairbridge Solent.

Terror in London

In the same year I was in the high court, London on a corporate fraud case lasting five days, when the red telephone alarm bell started ringing in the court. The Judge's clerk stood up to speak with the judge, and Counsel, in full flow, had to stop. The judge notified the court that there had been a terror alarm outside and the court's doors had to be closed. After some deliberation with the lawyers, including me, the judge said the case could go on, much to the relief of those involved. At the lunchtime break I telephoned Lizzie to see what had happened in London and she said the whole city, including transport, had to stop due to a terror threat. When we got to the end of the day, the court doors were opened and outside the atmosphere of London was so eerie it looked like something out of a John Wyndam, book with hundreds of people walking to their train stations and elsewhere. Cabs and buses were not running and, to add to the difficulties of the day, Waterloo was the only station open with trains running. Due to all of this, it was almost midnight when I got home.

A historical case of 'Trustees'

In December 2008, I was asked in the office to take up the case of Breakspear versus Ackland which was going to change the law of trusts which had been standing for four hundred years. My client was one of the claimants (Mrs Breakspear) and I had the help of a specialist trusts' barrister and queen's counsel (QC) The case went to the chancery division of the high court and took five days in the court room to be won for my client. It was a trust case about letters of wishes in wills. My client was a beneficiary under a family will. She sought an order of the court for the trustees to disclose the contents of a letter of wishes in the will. An earlier case named Londonderry's Settlement set the principle that the trustees are not accountable to the beneficiaries under their discretionary powers. In other words, they did not have to show the beneficiaries what is in the letter. After a five day battle in the court room, which we won by changing the law to make the general principle now to be that when a beneficiary applies to the court for disclosure of the letter of wishes the court does not have to do so other than for strong and legal reasons i.e. that the beneficiaries could ask to see the letter of wishes for 'legal reasons'.

Right up to the end of my career I continued to moot as a 'judge' to assist the weekly first year law students at Southampton University.

The next generation

As the grandchildren were growing up Lizzie and I became very useful as babysitters. They were particularly fond of Lizzie who, in a stroke of genius, created a dressing up basket full of clothes she no longer wore, which was immediately set-upon by them. On many occasions when they stayed, we would see or hear the grandchildren acting out their own made up play. Their efforts were sometimes very hilarious.

At other times we would take the grandchildren, Katie, Holly, Evie, Caliope and Daisy to the afternoon matinees at the local cinemas to watch Cartoons and films, such as *Alice in Wonderland*, amongst others and then treat them to a meal at, normally, TGI Fridays. We thoroughly enjoyed these outings and I in particular liked films such as *Madagascar*, with the psychotic penguins! On 9th July 2019 Katie gave birth to a boy named Bailey Hunter Gray Oakley making me a great-grandfather.

When the grandchildren were young, I said to my daughters, Emma and Anna, that they should enjoy them before they grew up, something my mother said to me.

On 26th July 2018, Emma married Christopher Hughes, a professional tennis coach. It was a wonderful wedding, including Emma's children Caliope and Daisy, plus many other families and friends.

As for Lizzie and me, we have now been together for more than twenty-six happy years — Love on forever!

Peter's sixtieth birthday, with (from bottom left),
Daisy, Caliope, Holly and Evie

Holly, Evie and Katie

Great-grandfather with Bailey, 2019

Epilogue

As a working-class boy, I chose law as a career for the people of Britain and society as a whole. Rightly, over the years, the courts became my love affair with justice. My passion was that of an ambitious go-getter and when I was with law students seeking a career in civil litigation, I told them there was no such thing as 'can't do'. On the contrary, a strong and worthy litigation lawyer would always be able to sail the client through the storms of problems, whether giving good or not-so-good news, the latter requiring comfort.

Following my legal fellowship in 1978, I became in 2000 a specialist litigation advocate in the higher courts. In doing that, I needed to have a clear mind like a kangaroo leaping. The judge and my professional opponent would be watching me all the time. The other people in the court would generally be my client, the client's opponent, the opponent's lawyer (if there was one), any witnesses, experts and the public, in a bench court. I digested all the salient points from both sides and, like an actor, delivered my cases succinctly and successfully. In so doing and over the years, I was helped by six firms of lawyers with the necessary types of litigation law I wanted to practise. Four of those headhunted me. As a result I helped many hundreds of people to get on with their lives without fear.

But let's go back. In the early days of my life, I listened to what my elders were saying to each other and what they were doing or not doing. This was the material I needed to build a picture of what was going on around me altogether throughout my life. On top of that, I wanted to know what was going on round the whole world to expand my knowledge, including languages. To do that I had to watch, look intently and listen very carefully.

At the age of five and when my parents went to the shopping centre of Southampton, still reeling with damage from the war, I watched the tractors and other vehicles going up and down the town making their busy noises throughout the day. In addition I watched men working in their trenches getting lots of mud on their boots. I was mesmerised by their images pounding through my life, as Southampton got up and built itself again, taking me with it as my home town.

As my younger years were going by quickly my enthusiasm brought me through schooling (educational and church), life boys, scouts and youth clubs up to my teens. A vision of how I came so far and delivered to my future was based upon the love and values of my mother and father. Having indulged in that, I never let them down. And by the way my parents never, ever had a car.

One of the best reasons for me being a go-getter was watching my great-grandfather, John Warren, the mariner, on a film made in 1920 of Sir Thomas Lipton's racing vessel, *Shamrock* being towed by a tug down the Itchen River, Southampton, in preparation for the start of the American's Cup and ending at Sandy Hook, USA. I was very excited that one of my family had taken part in such an awe-inspiring and worldly adventure. That was bolstered by Claude Graham-White's night flight. These images, given to me by my grandparents, inspired me for my future as an adult. By the way, Sir Thomas Lipton was a tea baron.

The losses of my beloved wife, Gloria at the age twenty-nine and my brother Paul, at the age of forty-three almost crushed me. Yet there was one certain thing that saved me, and that was life with my dear daughters, Emma and Anna. Despite very emotional decisions having to be made in the family, it was agreed that I take up the mantle of bringing up both girls. Thankfully, that worked out beautifully and I have two strong daughters and five granddaughters between them, all of whom I love with my heart. Even more my darling wife, Lizzie, saved me in the dark days following the loss of Paul.

A 1963 prize from my heart

In springtime 2019, I was looking through a pile of old papers and came upon an old blue textbook entitled *United States of America* and *P. Chainey*. Upon opening the inside lid I was met with the following: - '© 1963 P.C. Publications' and 'This book belongs to Peter Chainey, A. S. G. M. 35 Somerset Avenue, Harefield, Bitterne, Southampton'. There followed an 'Index' and 'The USA' with subtitles 'Page' 'Subject' and 'Dates' matched as page '1 to 51' and subjects of 'The birth', 'Civil War', 'The West and its History', 'Memorable dates', 'The North American Indian', 'The West to the Present Day', 'The States, (maps included)' and 'The Forms of Government'

The first page and line start with, 'A History of the United States of America' and 'The birth', followed with 'Have you ever thought why part of North America calls itself the United States? Or for that matter how those states first came to be united?' It ends with the *Battle Hymn of the Republic* and a separate picture of a pencil drawn American boy scout canoeing out of the book.

My manuscript was handwritten with blue biro and pencil for the drawings to make it's eighty pages easy to read. I wrote the book when I was fifteen, a good fifty-six years ago and it was my first book.

Winchester Cathedral

I have a great affection for Winchester Cathedral, having lived next to it for nine years. It is a towering Middle-ages cathedral housing the remains of many kings long gone. Although it looks monumental on the outside, it is warming and calming inside to give visitors a quiet place to repose, both physically and mentally. The choir is one of the best in the world and in the evening, I would sit against the wall to hear them singing.

One day in the 1980s, when I was cleaning my windows two American ladies asked where the bathroom was (as they do, meaning a toilet). The elderly lady wanted to go and spend a penny, so I said they could use my downstairs toilet. Whilst the older lady was doing what she had to do, I took the younger lady to look out the back window. With a tongue in cheek, I said, "Do you like the back garden?" and then "the garden shed," pointing at the cathedral. With a big laugh the younger woman said, "You're having me on." With that I entertained both ladies with a cup of warm English tea and biscuits, followed with a history of the cathedral, as a gesture of friendship.

Historically, the Lime trees in the Cathedral grounds were planted in the mid-eighteenth century. But in 1985 the trees were removed and replanted with re-twigged lime trees, due to decay on the older trees. Mainly, they act as ecological habitats for many creatures, plants and organisms with a visual line towards the cathedral. During the replanting of the trees, I looked out of my bedroom window and saw a man dig into the ground with 'mud on his boots'.

Note: These solicitors gave me the stepping stones for my career to be a qualified Lawyer:

1. Stephens Locke & Abel — 1964 – 1967, three years
2. Page Gulliford & Gregory — 1967 – 1971, four years
3. Bryan Colenso — 1971 –1973, two years
4. Shenton Pitt Walsh & Moss — 1973 – 1985, twelve years
5. Bernard Chill & Axtell — 1985 – 2003, eighteen years
6. Paris Smith & Randall — 2003 – 2012, nine years

Post script

In April 2018 I was told that I had mixed Alzheimer's disease and vascular dementia, following a diagnosis of dementia in October 2017. This is another challenge for me and one of the reasons I wanted to write this book. I love my life, my wife, my daughters, granddaughters, relatives and other close friends. On top of that I joined Eastleigh Fusion Choir as a singer to bring back memories of my singing days and to let me know, 'the music still goes on'.

Gallery

THE INSTITUTE OF LEGAL EXECUTIVES
Southampton and District Branch

Annual Luncheon

SOUTHAMPTON PARK HOTEL
CUMBERLAND PLACE
SOUTHAMPTON

THURSDAY, 8th NOVEMBER, 1984.
12.15 p.m. for 12.45 p.m.

———

Chairman:
Peter Chainey, Esq., F.Inst.L.Ex.

NATIONAL ASSOCIATION OF BOYS' CLUBS

17 BEDFORD SQUARE, LONDON, W.C.1   Telephone & Telegrams: Museum 5357

1 May 1967

Peter Chainey (Moorhill YC)

Two poems

"The Flower that through" - etc is the more striking of
these two poems.   It has an ingenious metre which gives
the poem significance, and some clever internal rhyming.
Its use of language is careful and the ideas imaginatively
expressed.

Silver and Bronze Awards

Edward McFadyen.

Peter Chainey. Age 19

Moorhill Youth Club 1967.

Spring 1985

City Bridge is the official journal of The Winchester Incorporated Chamber of Commerce. It is published periodically from the Chamber's office: 4 Chesil Street, Winchester SO23 8HU. Telephone Winchester 66294. Contents are copyright and may not be reproduced without prior permission.
Cover picture by Tony Chuter.

Editor: Peter Chainey.

Advertising: Colette Sandys (Winchester *EXTRA*, Tel. (0256) 461131)
Printed by Bird Brothers Ltd., Pelton Road, Basingstoke, Hants.

WINCHESTER INCORPORATED CHAMBER OF COMMERCE

President:
PETER LONGHURST
(Telephone Winchester 880274)

Deputy President:
NEVILLE WADE
(Telephone Winchester 884000)

Vice-President:
Mrs. W. LEWTAS
(Telephone Winchester 61865)

Chairman – Executive Committee:
NEVILLE WADE

Chairman – Retail Committee:
Mrs. W. LEWTAS

Chairman – Traffic and Planning Committee:
Mrs. S. KIDD
(Telephone Winchester 65966)

Treasurer:
ARTHUR CHANTLER
(Telephone Winchester 66666)

Secretary:
Mrs. G. A. WOOLDRIDGE
4 Chesil Street, Winchester SO23 8HU
(Telephone Winchester 66294)

Who inspires you the most?

My Grandad

By Caliope Neal

A little bit about them...

- DOB: 4th January 1948

- Where was he brought up? Bitterne, Southampton

- Job: Lawyer

- Nationality: British

- Family connection: my grandfather on my mother's side.

How are they inspirational?

My grandad has been through some difficult times in his life, but despite this he has always remained strong and positive. He lost his wife very early and had to raise my mum and her sister on his own. While raising two small children, he studied and qualified to become a lawyer in evening classes. He suffered a heart attack just before Christmas last year and was under a lot of stress while retiring.

He is inspirational to me because...

...he is always positive, no matter what he goes through. He is the happiest and most smiley person I have ever met. He always has a story to tell, whether it be funny or factual. I would very much like to be like my grandad, he has done well in his life and he lives life to the full. He loves music and film and as soon as he retired he started telling our family about all the things he wants to do. He wants to act, and he is also writing two books, one about his life and the other about being a lawyer.

I chose my grandad because...

...I think he is an amazing person. Everyone should be as positive as him. He makes me smile all the time and he really is inspirational. I am so proud of my grandad because I have never known anyone to be as strong as him.

LOVE YOU GRANDAD!

xxx

In Memory of

Private

Fred Chainey

31550, 15th (Hampshire Yeomanry) Bn., Hampshire Regiment who died on 14 October 1918 Age 21

Son of Mr. F. W. and Mrs. E. J. Chainey, of 71, Clarence St., Northam, Southampton.

Remembered with Honour
Dadizeele New British Cemetery

Commemorated in perpetuity by
the Commonwealth War Graves Commission

Paris Smith

Our People

Peter Chainey
Chartered Legal Executive Advocate

Peter is a very experienced Chartered Legal Executive Advocate in the Commercial Civil Litigation/Dispute Resolution Department. His long experience of 40 years in the law covers every aspect of commercial and other disputes including corporate fraud, intellectual property, building/construction, professional negligence, defamation, land law and personal injury.

Peter is a Past Chairman and Founder of the Southampton Civil Litigation Group and published author.

In a profile of 10 lawyers published by the Independent on Sunday in 2002 Peter featured as having climbed the ladder in law with "mud on his boots".

Contact for

Construction Disputes/Adjudications
Defamation

Contact Information
t. 023 8048 2415
f. 023 8048 2366
e. peter.chainey@parissmith.co.uk

Mr. G. Howe-Piper

Courtesy Call upon the Mayor of Southampton

Friday, 1st June, 1984.

11-25 am   The Mayor to receive in the Parlour :

              The Sheriff (Councillor G.M. Ranger)
              The Chief Executive (Mr. E.A. Urquhart)
              The Mayor's Chaplain (The Revd. B.J. Hartnell)

11-30 am   The Mayor and party to move to the Reception Room
              to receive representatives of :

Southampton City Magistrates

*	Mr. W.K. Struthers, JP	Deputy Chairman of the Bench
	Mr. H.J. Atkins, JP	Deputy Chairman
	Mrs. B.A. Martin, JP	Deputy Chairman
	Mr. H.R. Heath, JP	Deputy Chairman
	Mr. K.C. Clarke	Clerk to the Magistrates

The Institute of Legal Executives (Southampton and District Branch)

*	Mr. Peter Chainey	Chairman
	Mr. Ray Wedge	Vice Chairman
	Mrs. J. Dulford	Committee
	Mrs. L. Castleman	Committee
	Mr. Robert Kerr	Committee
	Mrs. J. Willingham	Secretary

The Rotary Club of Bitterne and Woolston

*	Mr. G. Howe-Piper	President
	Mr. P.L. Felton	Senior Vice President
	Mr. H.J. Sparshatt-Worley, JP	Junior Vice President
	Mr. K. Wiseman	Hon. Secretary
	Mr. D. Williams	Hon. Treasurer
	Mr. P.T. Exley	Immediate Past President

              Refreshments to be offered (0/9882)

   *   Greetings to be offered to the Mayor

              The Mayor to respond

12-15 pm   The guests to take their leave of the Mayor,
approx.   Sheriff, Chief Executive and the Mayor's Chaplain